AF358505

Constitutional Challenges
to the Drug Law
-A Case Study-

Roar Mikalsen

"A little rebellion
now and then
is a good thing."

— Thomas Jefferson—

CONTENTS

Introduction

IN THE HISTORY OF American jurisprudence, there have been more than 100 constitutional challenges to the drug law. This study presents an overview of the justice system's treatment of these challenges. It provides an analysis of the logic that judges have relied upon to dismiss the appellants' arguments and shows how the courts have failed to properly apply the Constitution whenever challenges to the drug law have been made.

As the U.S. Constitution established a system of law built on first principles, much of the focus will be on the qualitative difference that separates principled from unprincipled reasoning. As shall be seen, we are dealing with two different legal paradigms, one superior to the other, and nowhere is this better exposed than in challenges to the drug law. While unprincipled reasoning is quickly revealed to be the result of confused analysis and incomplete understanding—that is, as not being supported by any valid foundation—principled reasoning has as its defining trait that it is always harmonious with reason, leading back to first principles.

For purposes of constitutional construction, making out this distinction is particularly important. These two types of reasoning form the basis of any dispute on legal interpretation and *only principled reasoning* can accurately decipher the Constitution.

If this is so, one may ask why American judges so often have relied on unprincipled reasoning whenever challenges to the drug law have been made. Unfortunately, as I am here merely making available a case study that otherwise may go unnoticed, I must refer to my former book *To Right a Wrong*[1] for a more elaborate discussion on this topic. However, the short answer seems to be that we live in a society where drug policy to this day has been formed by prejudice and passion, and because so many judges are captured by the myth of the "demon drugs" psychological incentives ensure that they will want to protect the status quo. The only way to protect the status quo is to embrace unprincipled reasoning—and so, as long as their loyalty remains to the status quo rather than first principles, this is what they must do.

Even so, there will always be some who refuse to let pre-disposition and passion inform the system of law, and these judges will ensure that their argument is consistent with the implications of first principles. As shall be seen, however, these judges are a minority. They will express their opinions in dissents and their attempts to add to the integrity of the legal system have had no impact on the evolution of law.

As the credibility of the system depends on the extent to which judges prefer principled to unprincipled reasoning, this is highly unfortunate. Nevertheless, while the legal system to this day has failed to properly protect American citizens from a system of arbitrary law, the reasoning that has sustained the status quo speaks for itself, and by exposing it my hope is that Americans will see the sense in recognizing their founders' system of law.

---

[1] MIKALSEN, *TO RIGHT A WRONG: A TRANSPERSONAL FRAMEWORK FOR CONSTITUTIONAL CONSTRUCTION* (2016). This case study corresponds to its Part three and so there may be occasions where the reader would like further substantiation or more elaboration regarding certain claims or topics. If this is so, what you are looking for will be found in this book.

1

THE LAW &
CONSTITUTIONAL
CHALLENGES

"To rob the public, it is necessary to deceive it. To deceive it, it is necessary to persuade it that it is being robbed for its own benefit, and to induce it to accept, in exchange for its property, services that are fictitious or even worse."[2]

—Frederic Bastiat—

WHEN A LITIGANT WANTS to try the constitutionality of a law, he or she will either claim a due process or equality rights violation—or sometimes both. In the area of Due Process challenges, the modern doctrines of American law separate between fundamental rights and mere liberty interests; the fundamental rights will be those rights explicitly mentioned in the Bill of Rights and those dozen or so unenumerated rights that the courts have recognized as being of such importance that they qualify for protection anyway. In the area of equal protection challenges, the courts will target laws that attack groups on the basis of traits such as race, alienage, national origin, or sex; if a litigant claims an equal protection

---

[2] SCHALER (ED.), *DRUGS: SHOULD WE LEGALIZE, DECRIMINALIZE OR DEREGULATE?* (1998) 198

violation on these grounds the courts will review the matter, but only then.

Thus, modern doctrines will provide certain people with protection against discriminatory practices and they provide protection against infringements of certain rights that are deemed fundamental. If these criteria are met, strict scrutiny is applied, and the appellant will find herself well protected. The burden of evidence will be on the government to show that the legislation is a reasonable and necessary enterprise. This means that it will be for the state to demonstrate that it serves a compelling interest, that it is narrowly tailored to serve this interest, and that its objectives could not be met by relying on less restrictive means. If the courts, however, decide that these criteria are not met, then a presumption of constitutionality applies, and the burden of evidence will be on the appellant to convince the courts that there can be no conceivable legitimate reason for the law. This burden of proof has proven impossible to shoulder and the government wins no matter what.

While this is somewhat of a simplification,[3] this is the essence of the courts' approach to constitutional challenges, and we shall now, by example of drug policy, see how it makes a mockery of the founders' system of law.

---

[3] Due to obvious problems with this all-or-nothing approach to rights protection, the Supreme Court has more and more abandoned it. To fill in the blanks left by these two options, it will sometimes apply forms of scrutiny that can be placed somewhere in between these two extremes. This will be what has been called "rational basis review with bite," intermediate, or heightened review. Even so, as we shall see, the courts will use its fundamental rights doctrine to get the results that it wants.

1.1. The Way Forward
in a Principled System of Law

In the history of the drug laws there have been more than a hundred constitutional challenges.[4] The majority has focused on the legality of laws criminalizing the production, possession, use, or sale of the marijuana plant (or derivatives thereof) and together these challenges cover a broad spectrum of constitutional protections. In the area of equal protection challenges, appellants have argued that the scheduling system that categorizes illegal drugs is arbitrary and irrational. As regards to marijuana its status as a Schedule I drug has been challenged on the premise that neither the plant nor its derivatives satisfy the three statutory criteria necessary for inclusion in this category: (a) high potential for abuse; (b) no currently accepted medical use; and (c) lack of accepted safety for use of the drug under medical supervision. Litigants have provided substantial scientific evidence showing that none of these criteria apply and they have noted that the drug law was not properly framed. They claim that it is over-inclusive because the law punishes cannabis users as harshly as it punishes more harmful substances, like cocaine and heroin, and that it is underinclusive because the law fails to define similar punishments for comparable substances, like tobacco and alcohol. The essence of their charge is that the criminalization of drugs must have some scientific basis and that if society is going to permit alcohol and tobacco, two very dangerous drugs with significant attendant harms, then, in light of current knowledge, there is no rational basis for prohibiting marijuana.

---

[4] See list, page 201.

Furthermore, the harms associated with marijuana being less significant than those associated with legally regulated substances, they have argued that its prohibition is not a valid exercise of the police power. They have held that their choice in drugs is important to them for religious, medical, and/or recreational reasons, and that unless the state can document that the law is a necessary or reasonable intrusion, drug prohibition constitutes a violation of their right to autonomy, liberty, property, and the pursuit of happiness. They have claimed the protection of the First Amendment because the ingestion of these substances involves the reception of information or ideas (sometimes deeply spiritual in nature) and because "the State cannot, consistently with the spirit of this Amendment, unduly contract the spectrum of available knowledge."[5] They have claimed the protection of the Eighth Amendment because the severity of the sentences for drug law violations is incompatible with its prohibition of cruel and unusual punishment. They have claimed the protection of the Ninth and the Tenth Amendment because these were intended to protect all unenumerated rights and to keep the government off their backs. And they have claimed the protection of the Fifth and the Fourteenth Amendment because the drug laws, failing to reflect a proportionate and reasonable application of the police power, violate the Constitution's Due Process and Equal Protection mandates.

These charges are by no means unheard-of. We know that from a principled perspective it does not matter if a right to use drugs is enumerated in the Constitution.[6] The founders

---

[5] *Grisvold v. Connecticut*, 85 U.S. at 484 (paraphrasing)

[6] As Chief Justice Marshall explained, the nature of our Constitution "requires that only its great outlines should be marked, its important objects designated, and the minor ingredients which compose those objects be deduced from the nature of the objects themselves." *McCulloch v. Maryland*, 4 Wheat. 316, 407 (1819)

wanted all rights equally protected and the Ninth and Tenth Amendment were intended to ensure that the people retained their freedoms. No doubt, then, drug users—just as everyone else—have a right to challenge the constitutionality of a law that targets them for persecution. An effective remedy is at the core of the courts' mandate, and the issue brought before the courts is not some insignificant matter to be treated lightly—it is not about a "right to get high." As Professor Husak has noted, each year more persons are jailed or imprisoned for drug offenses than were jailed or imprisoned for all other crimes combined in any year from 1920 to 1970.[7] More than 40 million Americans have suffered incarceration. Every year 1.5 million more are caught in the net of the criminal process, and an additional 40 million annual drug users are up for grabs.[8] The ordeal directly associated with incarceration is just one aspect of the many consequences of the drug law, as violators will have to live the rest of their lives as second-class citizens, being ineligible for social security, student loans, as well as hundreds of other government programs. Many will also lose the right to vote and as a result more than 1.4 million Afro-Americans currently have no say in the electoral process. Add to this the disastrous effects that incarceration and other hardships have on their families (25 percent of African Americans who grew up in the past three decades have had at least one parent locked up) and we may begin to appreciate why philosophers of law have labeled drug prohibition "the worst injustice

---

[7] Husak, *Liberal Neutrality, Autonomy, and Drug Prohibitions* (2000)

[8] Even though blacks and other minority groups use these drugs no more often than white people, blacks are six times more likely to be the victims of these laws. As a result the United States, per capita, imprisons seven times as many of its black citizens as South Africa, the most racist regime in modern history, did under Apartheid. BECKER, *TO END THE WAR ON DRUGS* (2014) 18

perpetrated by our system of criminal law in the twentieth century,"[9] why judges have named it "the biggest failed policy in the history of our country, second only to slavery,"[10] and why also policemen have held the same.[11]

The consequences at the level of society underscores this point as drug prohibition has left a market worth more than $300 billion to be exploited by organized crime. As this force cannot exist without a comparable corruption of government,[12] it is difficult to overestimate the corruptive influence of the drugs economy. According to law enforcement experts, the political leadership in more than 30 countries is actively involved in the drugs economy.[13] There is much to suggest that this includes the leadership in America,[14] and that even in Washington DC. "no aspirant wins a high elective office

---

[9] HUSAK, *LEGALIZE THIS!* (2002) 5

[10] Judge James P. Gray in BECKER, *TO END THE WAR ON DRUGS* (2014) 36

[11] Norm Stamper, *Legalize Drugs—all of Them*, LA Times, December 4, 2005 ("It is not a stretch to conclude that our Draconian approach to drug use is the most injurious domestic policy since slavery.")

[12] As U.S. Chief Justice Earl Warren noted: "Organized crime can never exist to any marked degree in any large community unless one or more of the law-enforcement agencies have been corrupted. This is a harsh statement, but I know that close scrutiny of conditions wherever such crime exists will show that it is protected. ... The narcotics traffic . . . could never be as pervasive and open as it is unless there was connivance between authorities and criminals." Earl Warren, addressing the Milton S. Eisenhower Symposium, Johns Hopkins University, Baltimore, Maryland, Nov. 13, 1970

[13] MILLS, *THE UNDERGROUND EMPIRE* (1986)

[14] SCOTT, *AMERICAN WAR MACHINE* (2014); MARTIN, *THE CONSPIRATORS* (2002); GRITZ, *A NATION BETRAYED* (1989); MENASHE, *PROFITS OF WAR* (1998); REED & CUMMINGS, *COMPROMISED: CLINTON, BUSH AND THE CIA* (1994); STICH, *DEFRAUDING AMERICA* (1988); KWITNY, *THE CRIMES OF PATRIOTS* (1987); RUPPERT, *CROSSING THE RUBICON* (2004); O'BRIEN, *TRANCE-FORMATION OF AMERICA* (1995); RUSSELL, *DRUG WAR* (2000); MAZUR, *THE INFILTRATOR* (2009)

today without depending, directly or indirectly, knowingly or not, on crime-generated funds."[15]

It is beyond the scope of this book to describe the destructive consequences of drug prohibition. However, its constitutionality has been contested in academic circles since the 1960s,[16] and so one would expect the courts to give the issue its due consideration. Drug policy historians, after all, have carefully documented the trail of lies, deceit, prejudice and misconceptions that preceded, enveloped, and followed the legislative process in this period. It has been established that before the drug laws there was no real drug problem in

---

[15] Rufus King said this after having conducted an American Bar Association study on the drug laws (the Committee on Narcotics and Alcohol, Section of Criminal Law). MILLER, *THE CASE FOR LEGALIZING DRUGS* (1991) 71

[16] PACKER, *THE LIMITS OF THE CRIMINAL SANCTION* (1968) 333 ("A clearer case of mis-application of the criminal sanction would be difficult to imagine."); FULLER, *THE MORALITY OF LAW* (1969) 166 ("There is much reason to believe that our approach to the problem of drug prohibition is wrong, and that more would be achieved through medical and rehabilitative measures than through the criminal law."); Dichter, *Marijuana and the Law* (1968) 862 ("Since the use of marijuana, even for the mere enjoyment of the experience, is a form of expression dealing solely with the mind, a strong argument can be made for bringing this extremely private form of expression within the ambit of the zone of privacy surrounding the freedom of expression."); King, *Wild Shots in the War on Crime* (1971) 100-01 ("If a single folly. . . were to be selected as the worst, it would be the federal drug effort. . . . Uncle Sam has no business imposing criminal repressions in this field; what each citizen inhales, ingests, or injects into himself seems so far removed from the legitimate reach of any federal power that it is impossible to come up with a hypothetically *less* appropriate federal incursion."); Bonnie & Whitebread, *The Forbidden Fruit and the Tree of Knowledge* (1970) 1149 ("we believe that our central objection to the marijuana laws is of constitutional dimensions. We believe that those laws are irrational."); KAPLAN, *MARIJUANA: THE NEW PROHIBITION* (1971) 2 ("The costs of the marijuana laws far outweigh their benefits and . . . a drastic change in our whole approach . . . is necessary to avoid a national tragedy of major proportions."); Brashear, *Marijuana Prohibition and the Constitutional Right of Privacy* (1975) 581 ("it could be argued that marijuana use provides new sources of belief and experience and is protected under the first amendment because it supplies these necessary preconditions to speech and expression."); Hindes, *Morality Enforcement Through the Criminal Law and the Modern Doctrine of Substantive Due Process* (1977)

America (except alcohol);[17] that the first drug laws were the result of powerful lobby interests,[18] moral panic, and a deeply flawed political process;[19] that it was motivated primarily by racism, ignorance and empire building, and that things have not improved since then.[20] They have documented how bureaucratic thrust and power-political incentives ensured that the enemy image of drugs became an addiction, one that politicians would embrace to win votes, bureaucrats would

---

[17] The history of drug prohibition follows this pattern: *First* comes policy of escalating the drug war *and then* comes the escalating drug problems. We have seen this time and again and many scholars have described it: "When the opening shots were fired, and for many of the early years of the war on drugs, there was no publically recognized drug problem. Racism was the prime reason for the initial half-century of the war on drugs. The war on drugs provided a venue for gratuitously punishing selected types of people while providing a rationale that one was really doing good. It enabled sadism without guilt or embarrassment, without legal or public censure." Jerry Mandel, *The Opening Shots of the War on Drugs*, in FISH (ED.), *HOW TO LEGALIZE DRUGS* (1998) 213; ALEXANDER, *THE NEW JIM CROW* (2011) 5-6; BECKER, *TO END THE WAR ON DRUGS* (2014) 55; DUKE & CROSS, *AMERICA'S LONGEST WAR* (1993) 5; WISOTSKY, *BEYOND THE WAR ON DRUGS* (1990) 185

[18] "The elimination of marijuana came from pressures exerted by newly created 'Federal drug control agencies, cotton and timber interests, and chemical industries.'" *Seeley v. State*, 132 Wash. 2d 776, 940 P.2d 604 (1997) Footnote 10 (Sanders J., dissenting)

[19] In their seminal work Professors Bonnie and Whitebread summarizes their findings: "We have found no indication that the legislators consulted scientific data; instead they relied on sensationalistic police and newspaper identification of marijuana with crime. Naturally these assumptions went unchallenged; the only segment of the public likely to challenge them was small and outside the public opinion process." Bonnie & Whitebread, *The Forbidden Fruit and the Tree of Knowledge* (1970) 1166

[20] BAKALAR & GRINSPOON, *DRUG CONTROL IN A FREE SOCIETY* (1998) 68 ("Looked at as a series of incidents, the history of social and legal responses to drug use . . . sometimes seems melancholy and haphazard. It is easy to find inadequate pharmacology, inconsistent ad hoc responses based on poor information, indulgence of passions and prejudices, including racism, in response to drug scares, institutional self-aggrandizement by narcotics police, and a fair amount of hypocrisy and corruption."); Christiansen, *A Great Schism: Social Norms and Marijuana Prohibition* (2010) 235 ("A law that millions of Americans already believe to be invalid will be considered even more so as people learn that it was not based on scientific research, but rather racial prejudice and social conditions peculiar to the 1930s.")

employ to enlarge their budgets, and war profiteers would use to claim ever-increasing powers;[21] that because of these incentives public servants have consistently ignored all evidence of failure only to fuel the cycle of failure and escalation;[22] and that this has led to drug policies ever more detached from realities on the ground, ever more hostile to human flourishing, and increasingly opposed by a widening majority of experts.[23] In short, the history of drug prohibition shows that government has followed one imperative: to keep the War on Drugs going (and growing) at any cost, without

---

[21] WISOTSKY, *BEYOND THE WAR ON DRUGS* (1990) 173-74 ("It is difficult to find in modern American history an obviously defective and destructive policy so rigidly locked in place. A partial explanation for this unique rigidity lies in the fact that the ordinary corrective mechanisms that operate for some other failed governmental policies do not function here. First, the lack of even a minimal standard of performance by which to measure results precludes responsible dialog within the government. Without real goals there can be no accountability. Not once in the history of the War on Drugs . . . has the Government ever stated a realistic objective. . . . Second, the Government has effectively immunized itself from outside criticism, managing to preempt any serious public debate calling into question the premises of drug enforcement policy.") For more on why our public servants ignore all evidence of failure and instead make everything worse, see BERTRAM, ET AL., *DRUG WAR POLITICS: THE PRICE OF DENIAL* (1996) 102-62; WISOTSKY, *BEYOND THE WAR ON DRUGS* (1990) 173-97; BARNETT, *THE STRUCTURE OF LIBERTY: JUSTICE AND THE RULE OF LAW* (2014) 135-337; MILLER, *THE CASE FOR LEGALIZING DRUGS* (1991) 85-107; MILLER, *DRUG WARRIORS AND THEIR PREY* (1996) 164-69; EPSTEIN, *AGENCY OF FEAR* (1990) Husak, *Liberal Neutrality, Autonomy, and Drug Prohibitions*, (2000) 80 ("If the 'war on drugs' is unjustifiable, why does it continue to be waged? No single answer can be given. An important factor, however, is the financial gain to law-enforcement agencies that assign a high priority to the apprehension of drug offenders.")

[22] After looking through the systemic studies compiled by the National Commission on Marijuana and Drug Abuse, Epstein concluded that "none of the available data systematically gathered over a period of fifty years conformed to the . . . way politicians had used and abused the drug problem." EPSTEIN, *AGENCY OF FEAR* (1990) 268

[23] Galliher, Keys & Elsner, *Lindesmith v. Anslinger* (1998) ("Since the 1960s, few criminologists or criminal law professors have supported government drug policies. To this day, those setting American drug policy continue to ignore expert legal, academic, and medical advice. In the academic community there is now a clear recognition of long-standing patterns of both the ineffectiveness of, and racism inherent in American drug law enforcement. Indeed, opposition to contemporary American drug control policy has become normative in the academic community.")

checks and balances—and that the harder this war has been fought, the greater the human causalities in its wake.[24]

While prohibitionists will disagree, all this has been documented. Not only have advocates of prohibition never proven the validity of their premises; reform activists have noted their unwillingness to engage in debate, and the diversity of literature that prohibitionists and reform activists each can draw upon to advance an argument suggests that this is no coincidence. At the very least it attests to the inherent weakness of the prohibition argument; while philosophers of law are at a loss to find anything of substance in this category,[25] scholars have documented how drug prohibition has continued to this day supported by nothing but false premises, distorted data, overt lies, and a massive propaganda effort.[26]

---

[24] FISH (ED.), *HOW TO LEGALIZE DRUGS* (1998) xvi. ("For decades the federal government—the President, the Congress, and the courts—as well as state governments, both political parties, and a wide array of extragovernmental forces have combined to stifle the expression of a simple truth: drug prohibition, and its instrument of oppression, the war on drugs, makes the drug problem worse rather than better by creating a giant black market."); DUKE & CROSS, *AMERICA'S LONGEST WAR* (1993) 159 ("the government goes to great efforts to keep Americans from understanding that most deaths from drug overdoses are the products of prohibition, not the intrinsic qualities of the drugs themselves; that virtually all of the drug-related crime is the result of prohibition, not the pharmacological properties of the drugs; that the drug business as we know it is solely and entirely the consequence of prohibition. As a result, Americans attribute the evils of prohibition to illicit drugs themselves. The government calculatedly promotes such beliefs.")

[25] Husak, *Four Points about Drug Decriminalization* (2003) 23 ("[N]o case for criminalization has been adequately defended. It is utterly astonishing, I think, that no very good argument for drug prohibitions has ever been given. When I am asked to recommend the best book or article that makes a philosophically plausible case for punishing drug users, I am embarrassed to say that I have little to suggest.")

[26] ROBINSON & SCHERLEN, *LIES, DAMN LIES, AND DRUG WAR STATISTICS* (2007); BECKER, *TO END THE WAR ON DRUGS* (2014); SCHALER (ED.), *DRUGS: SHOULD WE LEGALIZE, DECRIMINALIZE OR DEREGULATE?* (1998); ESCOHOTADO, *A BRIEF HISTORY OF DRUGS* (1999); WISOTSKY, *BEYOND THE WAR ON DRUGS* (1990); DUKE & CROSS, *AMERICA'S LONGEST WAR* (1993); HART, *HIGH PRICE* (2014) 288-332; EPSTEIN, *AGENCY OF FEAR* (1990); FISH (ED.), *HOW TO LEGALIZE DRUGS* (1998); MILLER, *DRUG WARRIORS AND THEIR PREY* (1996) 3-33. Professor Barnett

This being so, one would expect the courts to be mindful of their responsibility to the Constitution, individual applicants, and the community at large. Considering that politicians have such a poor track record on this subject, one would expect the judiciary to step in and provide some quality control of a law that criminalizes 20 percent of the citizenry and of a war effort that scholars and law enforcement have described as a "totalitarian solution," a "vehicle for fascism,"[27] and a "lurch towards the police state."[28]

It is after all incontestable that drug prohibition from a liberal perspective is inherently suspect[29] and that there are especially weighty reasons for reviewing legislation that burdens politically marginalized groups. This, no doubt, includes drug users, as it is impossible to find a group against which government has been more antagonistically predisposed. Hence, as the justices at the Supreme Court have reminded us that "the very essence of civil liberty . . . consists in the right of every individual to claim the protection of the laws, whenever he receives an injury;"[30] "that experience

---

summarizes the prohibitionists' quest: "In war, it is said, truth is the first casualty. To be blunt, many committed prohibitionists inside and outside of government who profess to care so much about the morals of others routinely lie or willfully mislead the public about nearly every aspect of both drugs and the policy of prohibition. Our consistent experience with drug prohibition—from marijuana, to heroin, to cocaine—is that when careful empirical studies are eventually performed, they reveal the initial official accounts to be either false or wildly exaggerated. Rarely, if ever, does law enforcement then reverse itself or even moderate its rhetoric." Barnett, *Bad Trip* (1994) 2603. See also MIKALSEN, *TO END A WAR* (2015) endnotes 1, 14, 64, 66, 70

[27] MILLER, *THE CASE FOR LEGALIZING DRUGS* (1991) 118-24. Miller has even written a book on the subject. For more on how the drug warriors have completed four of the five steps in the chain of destruction identified by Holocaust-researchers (Identification—orstracism—confiscation—concentration—annihilation),   see MILLER, *DRUG WARRIORS AND THEIR PREY* (1996)

[28] MASTERS, *DRUG WAR ADDICTION* (2001) 29

[29] Buchhandler-Raphael, *Drugs, Dignity, and Danger* (2012)

[30] *Marbury v. Madison*, 5 U.S. 137 (1803) 163

teaches us to be most on our guard when the asserted Government purpose is to protect the public welfare";[31] that "it makes sense to scrutinize governmental action more closely when the State stands to benefit;"[32] and that "if it can be shown that one half of the effort has failed, we are at liberty to consider the question of policy with a freedom that was not possible before,"[33] we would expect them to honor their commitment to the rule of law.

The *only way* to do this would be to give the founders' system of principled law due recognition. And to ensure that the drug laws satisfy the criteria for constitutionality under a principled conception of rights, the Court must ask if the drug laws represent a necessary and proper application of the police power. To see if this is so, the Court has several modes of analysis available. It could go with the proportionality analysis that has risen to international prominence or it could go with domestically crafted models like the Lawton or Strict Scrutiny test. In either case the way forward is much the same: The state must show that the purpose for the law is legitimate; that the means it employs to reach this goal are necessary; that the law reflects a careful balancing of the interests of the individual and society; and that less restrictive means would not do.

To succeed in this endeavor, the state must show that the separation between licit and illicit drugs makes sense and that there are good reasons for criminalizing illicit drug users. The only way this can be done is by first demonstrating in specific

---

[31] *Olmstead v. U. S.*, 277 U.S. 438 (1928) 479 (Brandeis J., dissenting) (paraphrasing)

[32] *Bradley v. U. S.*, 410 U.S. 605 (1973); *Harmelin v. Michigan*, 501 U.S. 957 (1991) fn. 9

[33] Justice Holmes, *Common Carriers and the Common Law* (1879) 631

fashion the precise nature of the threat (i.e., the illicit drugs). After this, the state must show that the drug law is necessary to combat the threat; that it is effective in doing so; and that it at the same time preserves the interests of the individual and society. This means that the prohibition not only must be effective in curbing the supply and demand of the illicit drugs, but that it must be *the least intrusive* instrument amongst those which might achieve a protective function. *All these criteria must be met*, for only in doing so can it be said that the law strikes a fair balance between the rights of the individual and the interests of the community.

This is the essence of the test of reason, and if the state fails to show that the drug law satisfies these criteria, then we are dealing with an arbitrary, disproportionate, and discriminatory practice—and we have a violation of our catalogue of rights.

1.1.1. Considerations for the Court

Now, as we shall see, the courts have never looked into the premises of prohibition. Nevertheless, whenever citizens claim that constitutional rights are violated, they have a right to have the issue determined to the satisfaction of an independent, impartial, and competent court, and the first order of business for a court abiding by the rule of law would be to find out what exactly is the drug problem. For the goal of a drug free America to be legitimate, the state must show that the negative consequences of drug use outweigh the positive. The illicit drugs must be shown to pose a threat so tremendous that the world would be clearly better off without them and their alleged benefits must be shown to be trivial and negligible. To find out if this is so the court must examine why people take drugs, what it means to them, their patterns of use, and whether there can be valid reasons. It must investigate drug use from a historical and anthropological perspective as well as from a social and psychological point of view. Expert witnesses must be called upon to testify on these topics and what we can learn from history and common practices.

Traditionally, prohibitionists have had the privilege of defining the problem. However, their version of events has become increasingly contested, and so the court must find out if drug use really is the useless, misguided, dangerous, and inherently worthless pursuit that they claim. Relevant questions for consideration would be: Are drug users the maladjusted misfits they are portrayed to be? Do they use drugs merely for reasons of peer pressure, boredom, alienation, immaturity, depression, or some other pathology? Are they "victims of a plague who, tempted by pushers, peers, and the pleasures of drugs, succumb to the lure and lose control of themselves?"[34]

Is there some truth to this oft-cited prohibition-lore or does it vastly misrepresent the facts? Could the legalizers be correct in perceiving drug users as autonomous agents, people who normally handle themselves responsibly and consequently should be allowed to choose for themselves how to pursue their life-plan? Are they correct in asserting that most users are happy with their drug of choice, that they are functional citizens, and that they find drug use to be of value—a positive contribution to their life?

---

[34] SZASZ, *CEREMONIAL CHEMISTRY* (2003) 175 (paraphrasing)

Supposed that most people do describe their use in these terms, are they misguided? Do they misrepresent the truth, or could there be good reasons for using drugs? Is there evidence to suggest that their use could be a rational pursuit—one having inherent value? Assuming that there are benefits of drug use, what are they and how do they compare to harms? How many drug users experience the positive effects and how many experiences the harms? And when all is said and done, do the negative aspects of drug use overshadow the positive?

Furthermore, how do all of this relate to autonomy, the weightiest factor on the constitutional scale? Does drug use increase autonomy? Does it limit autonomy? Do the properties of certain drugs exact such a powerful influence that the concept of self-determination loses its meaning? Does drug use normally have a negative bearing on a person's ability to perform or contribute to society? Is it compatible with the rights of non-users to live free and productive lives? If it is not, in what sense does it conflict with the exercise of the fundamental rights of others? If drug use does negatively impact autonomy, what drugs are worse? How representative are the worst-case scenarios? And how do they compare with those instances of asserted/actual autonomy enhancement?

These are important questions to consider, but we have by no means neared the end of our quest. Before we can form an opinion on the drug problem, we must also ask: what part of it is prohibition related and what part is pharmacologically related? We know that many of the harms associated with drug use must be attributed to its criminalization; what are the actual costs of prohibition?

Another area of investigation must be whether the harms related to drug use are greater than the harms associated with other activities that we have learned to live with. After all, there is a risk associated with everything we do. Nothing is more lethal than living and so what is the risk-benefit ratio? When it comes to sports: Is drug use more dangerous than motorcycling, ski jumping, horse riding, mountain climbing, or other activities? When it comes to foods: Are the illicit drugs more harmful than peanuts, sugar, salt, fast-food, etc.? When it comes to the legal drugs: are the illicit drugs more dangerous than tobacco, alcohol, coffee, aspirin, valium, etc.? Are they more prone to be misused? Do their addictive and pharmacological properties render them especially problematic? And what about the user groups: Why exactly is it ok to persecute the former and not the latter? What crimes against fellowmen has a cannabis/cocaine user, producer, transporter, or distributor committed that alcohol drinkers, producers, transporters, or distributors have not? Are the former more prone to mischief? Have their involvement with these drugs stripped them of autonomy rights and human dignity? Have they debased themselves and lost their humanity? Are they no longer worthy of equal protection?

For drug prohibition to be sustained there must be something about the illicit drugs (other than their classified status) that makes their users worthwhile targets for the criminal law. A prime objective for the court therefore must be to find out why this group of people has been selected to bear the burden of the law. Is there a plausible, nonarbitrary explanation for this or does the classification merely reflect disproval, dislike, or stereotyping of the class of persons burdened by the legislation?

If any of these inquiries come up short, prohibitionists will already be on shaky ground. However, assuming that the harmful effects of drugs are unparalleled; assuming that they are vast and weighty compared to whatever positive qualities;

assuming that the positive qualities are of little significance—
and that we are qualified to make this value judgment on
behalf of others: Once we have established that the goal of a
drug-free America is a worthy endeavor, it must be shown to
be feasible. The relationship between means and ends is
profoundly significant whenever the question of constitutionality is addressed and the state must not only show that
drug prohibition serves important governmental objectives
but is substantially related to the achievement of those
objectives. This means that the price of pursuing the goal of
a drug-free America must not be too high and that the law
must be properly tailored to deal with the threat. Not only
must there be a relationship of proportionality between the
importance of reaching the goal and the price we can be
expected to pay for pursuing policy. There must also be a
reasonable relationship of proportionality between the ways
we deal with different threats—alcohol, tobacco, cocaine,
marijuana, etc.

So how have the drug laws served society? Has the
prohibition experiment functioned as intended? What has
been its effect on the supply and demand of illicit drugs? To
what extent has the criminal law been an effective deterrent?
To what extent has prohibition succeeded in reducing the
potential harms caused by drug use? To what extent are other
factors important? Has it proven efficient or are there fatal
flaws in the strategy that cannot be amended? Is a prohibition
the least drastic means available to deal with the problems of
drug abuse, or could we achieve the same—or better—results
by less despotic means? And what about the societal
consequences of prohibition: To what extent has the drugs
economy corrupted our social order? Are the good guys and
the bad guys clearly defined different groups, or has the illicit

economy corrupted society to the point where even governments are in on it?

If the latter is the case, how realistic is the goal of winning a War on Drugs? And if we add up all the negative consequences of drug use with all the negative consequences of prohibition, which one would come out on top? In the final balancing of scales, are the problems generated by drug use sufficiently serious to merit criminalization or is the remedy a bigger evil than the mischief it seeks to eradicate?

All these questions must be contemplated. The answers must be carefully weighed for the court to make sense of the larger picture and arrive at an informed opinion as to if the war effort is necessary. To find out if the law is a proper application of the police power it must always be necessary— and to be necessary, it must never be more invasive than needed to protect the public welfare. It must be effective in dealing with the mischief at hand and represent a careful balancing of the interests of the individual and society. As always, the liberty presumption favors the individual's right to choose her own life-plan and any doubt must be resolved in favor of liberty. This means that if less invasive means could contain the problem, they must be the preferred option and drug prohibition fails the test of reason.

1.2. The Way Forward
in an Arbitrary System of Law

We have just seen what it would entail if the state would ever have to defend its policies. However, most justices do not think this is necessary and when a constitutional challenge comes their way, they will find a way to disparage the rights claim. Depending on the charges levied against the law, the courts differ in their approach, but the gist of their argument is that "because there is no fundamental constitutional right to import, sell, or possess illegal drugs," they will defer to the legislative and uphold the legislation.[35]

Some courts have been more hostile to the rights claim than others, but the standard approach for denying drug use status as a protected right is simple. The court will begin its analysis by stating that "in ascertaining whether a right is fundamental, a court must determine whether the right is explicitly or implicitly guaranteed by the Constitution." Looking at this, drug use is not explicitly protected and so the question becomes: is it implicitly protected?

So far in the analysis both advocates of a principled system of law and an arbitrary system of law agree—and from here on the proper way forward would be to recognize the individual's autonomy and liberty interest and perform a balancing test as to whether the interests of society outweighs the interests of the individual. This is what those who adhere to the founders' system of law will do. However, because most judges mistake the spirit of the Constitution with its letter and prefer to go with precedent and tradition rather than principled thinking, they choose another route.

This is what comes natural to them. For one, as shown in *To Right a Wrong*, there is a difference that separates those who will reason from a principled perspective and those who will not. Psychologically speaking, they are at different stages of growth, and while only a minor percentage of the

---

[35] For a few representative cases, see *Raich v. Gonzales*, 500 F.3d 850 (9th Cir. 2007); *Nat'l Org. for Reform of Marijuana Laws (NORML) v. Bell*, 488 F. Supp. 123 (D.D.C. 1980); *United States v. Kiffer*, 477 F.2d 349 (2d Cir.); Louisiana Af. of NORML v. Guste, 380 F. Supp. 404 (E.D. La. 1974); *State v. Mallan*, 86 Haw. 440, 950 P.2d 178 (1998)

population (roughly 10 percent) have advanced normatively and cognitively to the point where they are sufficiently free from contemporary constraints to connect with the light of first principles, the majority will remain too entangled in the mindset that connects them to their day and age.

While controversial, this has been well-established.[36] History is a testimony to the extent to which the masses are moved by prejudices, not reason, and accepting this is of crucial importance if we are to understand why some will prefer a system of arbitrary law to one of principled law. It is not that they will not officially endorse the latter, but they are simply too mired in the collective consciousness to see beyond society's mores. Hence, because most judges are at a level of growth where they remain bound by contemporary constraints, they have no access to the implications of first principles; they cannot fathom their reach; and they cannot see how they connect. Second, because they fail to connect with this bigger picture, they cannot see their day and age in a historical context; they cannot access the timeless world of universal morality; and they do not know how to work with a general conception of rights. Third, because they have no access to this greater framework of reasoning, they are in the position of blind leading the blind, and so they are naturally afraid of doing their job—which is to be moral arbiters and overturn acts of the legislature whenever politicians fail to properly respect individual boundaries.

Consequently, most judges will continue their analysis on this track: First, they will say that because "guideposts for responsible decision-making in this uncharted area are scarce and open-ended," (i.e., "because we do not know how to

---

[36] MIKALSEN, *HUMAN RISING: THE PROHIBITIONIST PSYCHOSIS AND ITS CONSTITUTIONAL IMPLICATIONS* (2018)

operate within the territory of principled law") and because "judicial extension of constitutional protection for an asserted right places the matter outside the arena of public debate and legislative action," (i.e., "because we have no better guidance than the irrational movement of the masses") they will defer to the legislature whenever possible.

To find out if deference is an option, they must make sure that the asserted right in question is a mere liberty interest and not a fundamental right, for if they can conclude with the former their business is done. Never mind that the founders wanted all rights equally protected. Never mind that the separation between liberty interests and fundamental rights is an arbitrary divide. Never mind that this mode of analysis outright defies the rule of construction specifically outlined by the Ninth Amendment: Because they do not know how to maneuver by first principles they must go by precedent. The past is the only map they know that will provide them with a sense of direction, and so the task will be to find out if the right in question is sufficiently similar to other, already accepted rights to merit protection.

When it comes to this, one more thing must be said of the psychological predisposition that characterizes people at the lower stages of growth. This is that they are much like children compared to adults, as only those at the higher stages will be psychologically disposed to embrace the obligations that come with social contract thinking. Depending on their personality, people at the lower stages of growth will either be inclined to rule others or to be ruled by others. In either case, they will be uncritically embracive of authoritarian systems and so most judges, true to their authoritarian bent, will demand a narrow description of the asserted right, which normally (depending on the constitutional challenge) will be the smoking of marijuana either for religious, recreational, or medical purposes. Thus, because they cannot operate at the level of principled reasoning (and the use of marijuana for these purposes is not explicitly mentioned in the Constitution), their psychological set-up ensures that these judges will determine the status of marijuana smoking by asking whether it is so "deeply rooted in this Nation's history and tradition," or so "implicit in the concept of ordered liberty" that neither liberty nor justice would exist if it was sacrificed.

Moreover, because this test is not rooted in any objective criteria, it will be up to the judge to arrive at a conclusion based on his own preferences, and after comparing marijuana smoking to other, already protected activities he is not likely to be impressed with the importance of protecting this right. Colored by many years of prohibitionist propaganda, he will be deeply suspicious (if not openly hostile) to any claim that this activity merits protection, and so the way forward is predictable. After looking at the rights claim, the judge will simply reaffirm his own prejudices, stating that "smoking marijuana receives no explicit or implicit constitutional protection;" that "the act of smoking does not involve the important values inherent in questions concerning marriage, procreation, or child rearing" (i.e., the other protected rights); that "its use predominantly as a 'recreational drug' undercuts any argument that its use is as important as, e.g., use of contraceptives;" and that it is neither so deeply rooted in this Nation's history and tradition nor so implicit in the concept of ordered liberty that freedom or justice would seize to exist if it was sacrificed. At this point in the analysis, the judge is likely to quote the *Ravin* court's speculation that "few would believe they have been deprived of something of critical importance if deprived of marijuana," and on this basis, he will conclude that "private possession of marijuana cannot be deemed fundamental."[37]

In the large majority of constitutional challenges brought before the courts, this is all the effort it takes for a judge to deny the argument any merit. He or she will simply quote previous court decisions while taking for granted that their analysis was properly performed. Only a very few courts have put in some effort on their own and one of them was the *Ravin* court. In the history of constitutional challenges this is one of the most important, as the Alaska Supreme Court held that the Alaska Constitution's right to privacy protects an adult's ability to use and possess a small amount of marijuana in the home for personal use. Unlike all the other courts that put the burden of evidence on the applicants, the *Ravin* court did not disparage marijuana smoking as an utterly insignificant activity. It recognized that the drug law represented a substantial intrusion into the sphere of privacy, and because "the privacy of the individual's home cannot be breached absent a persuasive showing of a close and substantial relationship of the intrusion to a legitimate governmental interest," it put the burden on the state to show that this was the case.[38]

After a careful review, the justices found "no firm evidence that marijuana, as presently used in this country, is generally a danger to the user or to others." And after weighing "the relative insignificance of marijuana consumption as a health problem," the importance of

---

[37] For this line of reasoning, see *United States v. Maas*, 551 F. Supp. 645 (D.N.J. 1982) at 647; *NORML v. Bell*, 488 F. Supp. 123 (D.D.C.1980) at 132-3

[38] As the court said: "Here, mere scientific doubts will not suffice. The state must demonstrate a need based on proof that the public health or welfare will in fact suffer if the controls are not applied." *Ravin v. State*, 537 P.2d 494 (1975) 511

respecting the sanctity of the home, and the importance of personal autonomy to the people of Alaska, the Court did not see the requisite "close and substantial relationship" between the state's asserted interest in protecting the public from marijuana use and the means chosen to advance that interest (a law prohibiting all possession and use of marijuana). Consequently, the Alaska Supreme Court became the first to provide constitutional protection for marijuana users.

Later courts, however, have disregarded this part of the *Ravin* court's analysis. They have explained it away by saying that the Alaska Constitution provides better privacy protection than other state and federal constitutions (as if that is at all possible), and instead of focusing on that aspect of the court's analysis which held privacy to be important and that the state must show some reasonable relationship between means and ends, they have cited *Ravin* for its fundamental rights analysis. This is highly unfortunate, for as we shall see its fundamental rights analysis was misframed and erroneous. Nonetheless, on the basis of its deeply flawed analysis later courts have jumped to the conclusion that no fundamental right to drug use exists, and this has been the end of any Due Process complaint.

In the area of Equal Protection challenges applicants have fared no better, for "in light of the very limited constitutional interests asserted by defendants," the courts think it "clear that they have not been denied equal protection of law."[39] Because most judges see marijuana use as a significant "threat to society as a whole,"[40] they have great difficulty considering the possibility that the Constitution provides such activity with meaningful protection and they see no reason

---

[39] *United States v. Bergdoll*, 412 F. Supp. 1308 (D. Del. 1976) at 1314

[40] *Borras v. State*, 229 So. 2d 244 (1969) at 246

why the state should have to justify its different treatment of marijuana smokers and alcohol drinkers. They make it clear that in this area the legislature has been granted a wide discretion in attacking social ills and that "if Congress decides to regulate or prohibit some harmful substances, it is not thereby constitutionally compelled to regulate or prohibit all."[41]

Due to this policy of legislative freedom in confronting social problems, the courts have declined to investigate if there is a rational basis for treating the different groups of drug users differently. Not only that, but because of the perceived unimportance of the asserted right, courts "do not agree with the defendants that the Legislature is bound to adopt the 'least restrictive alternative' that would fulfill its purpose of protecting the health, safety and welfare of the community."[42] In fact, because the right in question is perceived to be of so little importance, these judges "know of nothing that compels the Legislature to thoroughly investigate the available scientific and medical evidence when enacting a law. The test of whether an act of the Legislature is rational and reasonable is not whether the records of the Legislature contain a sufficient basis of fact to sustain that act. The Legislature is presumed to have acted rationally and reasonably,"[43] and this is true even if evidence to the contrary exists.

In other words, "every presumption is indulged in favor of the validity of a statute."[44] The legislature's decision to criminalize drug use may be contaminated with prohibitionist

---

[41] *United States v. Kiffer, supra,* 477 F.2d at 355

[42] *Commonwealth v. Leis,* 355 Mass. 189 (1969) at 195

[43] Id. 192

[44] Id. 200

prejudice, contradictory logic and demonstratively false presumptions—it does not matter. At this level of scrutiny there is no inquiry into the relationship between means and ends, no second-guessing of Congress's "wisdom, fairness, or logic of legislative choices,"[45] and the burden remains with the contender to show that there can be no conceivable rational basis for the legislative action. This has proven impossible, for as long as the state holds that the classifying measure is necessary no further explanation is needed.[46]

With very few exceptions, the courts that have considered the constitutionality of the drug laws have consistently applied this form of review. As a result, all these constitutional challenges have failed, and we shall now go into detail as to the reasoning that has been used to uphold drug prohibition.

---

[45] *Heller*, 509 U.S. 319

[46] As the *Pickard* court held: "Under the deferential standard of rational basis review . . . as long as there is some conceivable reason for the challenged classification of marijuana, the [drug law] should be upheld. Such a classification comes before the court bearing a strong presumption of validity, and the challenger must negative every conceivable basis which might support it. The asserted rationale may rest on rational speculation unsupported by evidence or empirical data. The law may be overinclusive, underinclusive, illogical, and unscientific and yet pass constitutional muster. In addition, under rational basis review, the government has no obligation to produce evidence to sustain the rationality of a statutory classification." *United States v. Pickard, et. al.*, No. 2:11-CR-0449-KJM (2015) 27-28 (citations and internal quotation marks omitted)

2

THE PROBLEMATICS OF UNPRINCIPLED REASONING

"It is of great importance to observe that the character of every man is, in some degree, formed by his profession. A man of sense may only have a cast of countenance that wears off as you trace his individuality, whilst the weak, common man has scarcely ever any character, but what belongs to the body; at least, all his opinions have been so steeped in the vat consecrated by authority, that the faint spirit which the grape of his own vine yields cannot be distinguished. Society, therefore, as it becomes more enlightened, should be very careful not to establish bodies of men who must necessarily be made foolish or vicious by the very constitution of their profession."[47]

—Mary Wollstonecraft—

THE CASE OF THE drug laws exposes the problematics of reasoning from a perspective of arbitrary law. Nowhere is its illogicality and deceptiveness better exposed, and nowhere is the injustice that follows in its wake more pronounced. We shall now discuss the various ways by which the courts set a challenge up for failure.

---

[47] WOLLSTONECRAFT, *A VINDICATION OF THE RIGHTS OF WOMEN* (1790) 17

2.1. Improper Deference

The first thing we may notice is that the courts use a presumption of legality to sustain the validity of the law. The defendants are never given a chance to defend themselves, as whatever evidence there exists to challenge the law is ignored. This, as Judge Shangler of the Michigan Supreme Court noted, "contradict[s] the principle that the constitutionality of a criminal statute predicated upon the existence of a particular state of facts may be challenged by showing to the court that those facts have ceased to exist."[48] In every challenge to the drug laws the appellants seek an opportunity to show that the present state of facts do not support prohibitionist assumptions, and as "[t]he determination that the classification remains justified . . . can only come after full consideration of the most contemporary and informative data,"[49] they are denied their day in court.

The right to an independent, impartial, and competent court is at the very heart of the right to a fair trial. And so, as a person cannot be imprisoned without being accorded a fair hearing in accordance with the Due Process Clause, the extreme prejudice with which these challenges is met is incompatible with constitutional protections.

Furthermore, not only do the courts deny appellants an opportunity to have the true state of facts determined but the courts' faith in the legislature is hardly warranted. Legislatures, after all, rarely act in accord with principle when they enact laws. The laws they enact usually come about as a result of lobbyism, peer pressure, or as a response to majoritarian will, and the principled reasoning that guides

---

[48] *State v. Mitchell*, 563 S.W.2d 18 (Mo. 1978) 34 (Shangler J., dissenting)

[49] Id. 35 (Shangler J.)

human rights thinking has nothing to do with either. In fact, human rights law is there to protect us from the despotism of special interests, bureaucracy, or populism. And so, as the legislature has not been known to examine if the laws they enact and uphold are compatible with its principles, the courts' presumption of legality is highly misplaced.

Another reason why the courts' deference violates the Constitution is that the burden of proving guilt naturally belongs to the state. Hence, as it is a constitutional requirement that the burden of proving guilt is placed squarely on the government, it is only logical that the burden of proving that the criminal law is compatible with constitutional limits should be placed there. After all, the question of guilt does not only depend upon whether a defendant has broken the law. The question of guilt goes further. It is fundamentally entwined with the judicial maxim that all punishment must be deserved, and as the principle of *just desert* (no punishment without moral culpability) reaches into the substantive areas of the law, the question of guilt depends on whether the law conforms to principles of justice.

Thus, the constitutional requirement that the burden of proving guilt remains with the government logically extends to constitutional challenges and the criminal law. As Justices Black and Douglas stated in their *Turner* dissent:

"It would be a senseless and stupid thing for the Constitution to take all these precautions to protect the accused from governmental abuses if the Government could by some sleight-of-hand trick with presumptions make nullities of those precautions. Such a result would completely frustrate the purpose of the founders to establish a system of criminal justice in which the accused . . . would be able to protect himself from wrongful charges by a big and powerful government. It is little less than fantastic even to imagine that those who wrote our Constitution and the Bill of Rights intended to have a government that could create crimes . . . and then relieve the government of proving a portion of them.

[If] Congress . . . define[s] a crime . . . due process requires the Government to prove *each element* beyond a reasonable doubt before it can convict the accused of the crime it deliberately and clearly defined."[50]

This is especially important in those "crimes" where no person is directly victimized. In instances such as this, where the government to justify punishment refers to such abstract notions as "harm to society," the burden of proving that the law conforms to principles of justice must not only befall the government, but the government must pass the compelling interest/strict scrutiny test. If not, the government will have the power to criminalize any behavior no matter how private or innocent. After all, most of our actions cause some indirect harm to some vaguely defined social interest. For example, sport activities—in fact, *any* activity—can result in physical injuries which again could be said to pose some degree of harm to society. Likewise, much of what we eat contains some harmful substances. Not only that, but all foods can be abused by overeaters, and, as all foods have the potential of making us less than healthy, the government could find an excuse for criminalizing these products. Furthermore, speech is often provocative and every day people say things that have the potential of indirectly harming some social "interest." It may strike at prejudices and biases and have profound

---

[50] *Turner v. United States*, 396 U.S. 398 (1970) (Black, J., with whom Douglas J. joins, dissenting.) (emphasis mine)

unsettling effects. In times of tyranny, for example, simply speaking the truth will be a revolutionary act and the government's interest in self-preservation can be used to justify any infringement on "objectionable" speech.

Now, the "harms" attached to sports, foods, and speech are quite different in nature. The first two are characterized by physical and economic harm, while the latter is usually thought of as a "moral" harm. The State is more likely to criminalize the latter, for it is willing to accept a great deal of physical and economic harm if it does not threaten the perceived values of the status quo (which means the power base of authority).

When our leaders talk of "harm to society," therefore, what they usually mean is a threat to their own perceived power base, and history leaves no doubt that this is the common denominator behind the "harms" our leaders are keen to eradicate. While they tend to accept (and encourage) any harmful activity as long as it is seen to promote their interests (power, prestige, and money), we see that any abstract and vaguely defined "harm" is to be dealt with as long as it is deemed threatening to the powers that be. Consequently, unless the government bears the burden of showing us that it has a compelling interest in criminalizing such behavior, there is no limit to the laws it may enact.

Now, this improper deference to the legislature is a consequence of the rational basis test, which again is an upshot of the fundamental rights doctrine. Scholars have criticized both for being incompatible with the spirit of the Constitution and in drug cases several judges have joined the choir. As Justice Sanders put it in his *Seeley* dissent:

"This two-tiered classification system of strict scrutiny and rational basis has proven problematic and subject to criticism because it shoehorns what in reality exists on a continuum into absolute but artificial categories. While the 14th Amendment simply references 'liberty,' the question posed by the majority is whether there is a 'fundamental interest' to smoke marijuana. I disagree with this formulation because the constitution speaks of principles, not specifics. Freedom from needless suffering; the right to individual autonomy; the right to bodily integrity . . . and freedom from arbitrary, privacy-invading restraints are the principles applicable here.

Better we should question the predicate which supposedly justifies state intervention in the first place than shift the burden to the private citizen to show why he should be free—which is, or should be, the natural state in a free society."[51]

This, of course, is principled reasoning, and to justices like Sanders it is clear that laws prohibiting the sale, use, and/or ingestion of marijuana are in violation of the Constitution. They have long held that First Amendment, Fifth Amendment, Eighth Amendment,[52] Ninth Amendment and Fourteenth Amendment rights are implicated in drug use. According to them, it is clear that *there is* a "fundamental constitutional right to smoke marijuana;"[53] "that it is founded

---

[51] *Seeley v. State*, 132 Wash. 2d 776, 940 P.2d 604 (1997) 631 (Sanders J., dissenting)

[52] Bonnie & Whitebread, *The Forbidden Fruit and the Tree of Knowledge* (1970) 1153 ("the rationality arm of the eighth amendment should prohibit imprisonment for violation of that legislation, even for five minutes")

[53] Justice Abe of the Hawaiian Supreme Court stated in 1972 that "I do not agree . . . that one does not enjoy the fundamental constitutional right to smoke marijuana. . . . I believe that the right to the 'enjoyment of life, liberty and the pursuit of happiness' includes smoking of marijuana, and one's right to smoke marijuana may not be prohibited or curtailed unless such smoking affects the general welfare." *State v. Kantner*, 493 P.2d 306 (1972) at 312 (Abe J., concurring)

upon the constitutional rights to personal autonomy and privacy, guaranteed by [the state and Federal] Constitution;"[54] that "our present method of regulating marijuana . . . is unreasonable and unconstitutional in violation of the due process and equal protection clauses of the Fourteenth Amendment;"[55] that the drug law therefore "violates the Federal and State Constitutions in that it is an impermissible intrusion on the fundamental rights to liberty and the pursuit of happiness, and is an unwarranted interference with the right to possess and use private property;"[56] and that "where the State endeavors to intrude into the individual's private life and regulate [such] conduct, . . . it is the duty of the courts to offer a haven of refuge where the individual may secure vindication of his right to be let alone."[57]

The only problem for drug users, then, is that individuals who reason from first principles are few and far between. In the history of challenges to the drug laws, we find them expressing their judgment in the dissents rather than the majority opinions. But even so, their reasoning speaks for itself and it is clear that "the majority's response is . . . misguided and in error."[58] Furthermore, the self-defeating reasoning relied upon by the majority suggests that it only "seeks a legal shield behind which it can avoid objective

---

[54] Id. 313 (Levinson J., dissenting)

[55] Id. 319 (Kobayashi, J., dissenting)

[56] *People v. Sinclair*, 387 Mich. 91, 194 N.W.2d 878 (1972) 133 (Kavanagh J., concurring)

[57] *Kantner*, 493 P.2d 306 (1972) 317-18 (Levinson J., dissenting)

[58] *State v. Mitchell*, 563 S.W.2d 18 (1978) 29 (Seiler J., dissenting)

inquiry,"[59] and that the rational basis test and fundamental rights analysis is their way of doing so.

For reasons discussed in *To Right a Wrong* (and which will be further explained), most judges will have strong objections against letting drug users have their day in court. Reason, however, will not come to their rescue and to disparage the rights-claim, they must rely on a variety of phony tactics.

These shall now be reviewed.

2.2. Mistaking Shadow and Light

The most common way for courts to deny drug users a fair trial is by a failure to recognize that the enumerated rights are a shadow that is cast by the light of more fundamental principles. We have seen that according to the founders' idea of rights, it does not matter if rights are enumerated. The unenumerated rights are just as important as those spelled out, but most judges, being oblivious to the bigger and how it connects, only focus on the enumerated rights. Thus, they will perform an analysis that betrays an ignorance of the ideas upon which the American system is built. This ignorance is made explicit by such statements:

> "Plaintiffs' claim in the present case rests on bare allegations of a general right to privacy to do what one wishes in his own home and with his own body. Although plaintiff does claim enforcement of this right of privacy through the Fifth and Fourteenth Amendment and through the Ninth Amendment, he does not ground it or

---

[59] Id. 29 (Seiler J., dissenting)

even attempt to ground it on any one of the amendments which protect certain guaranteed rights and which in doing so create constitutionally guarded zones of privacy."[60]

As discussed previously, the right to privacy is not explicitly stated in the Constitution. Even so, it is recognized that zones of privacy are created by the penumbras of the first, third, fourth, fifth, and ninth amendments, and the objection in this case was that the appellant did not first attempt to ground his claim in one or more of these. A more telling example of the confused reasoning with which challenges to the drug laws are met is difficult to find, for if the judge did not have it backwards, he would have understood that plaintiff's failure to "ground it or even attempt to ground it on any one of the amendments" did not impair the argument. How could it? The amendments themselves are grounded in (and validated by) the underlying principles of law. These principles do not care if an activity is enumerated or whether it is similar to other activities already granted "fundamental" status. All they do is establish that the individual is to be given a free rein and that any limitation to his domain must be justified by sufficiently weighty considerations. That is all. The central issue is autonomous choice, and whether you, I, or the government, would think it wise is irrelevant.

Looking at the relationship between these principles and the enumerated rights, the right to privacy is more closely connected to these principles than the amendments. The light of these abstract principles is channeled into a more "tangible" right to privacy, which again provides context and substance to the few enumerated rights. Thus, it obviously

---

[60] *Louisiana NORML v. Guste*, 380 F. Supp. 404 (1974) 407

makes no sense to ask the appellants to ground their claim in the latter. The legalization argument remains firmly grounded in the principle of autonomy—the underlying principle that has given validity all the enumerated rights (as well as the right to privacy), and this being the case, it is absurd to ask the appellants to look for it elsewhere.

The example above was District Judge Comiskey's reply to a legal challenge made by the law reform organization NORML in 1974.[61] Comiskey's response, however, is not unique. It represents the norm, and six years later, when NORML countered the drug law with another challenge, they were met with the same reaction. In an effort to ground the rights-claim in precedent NORML's lawyers had relied on *Stanley v. Georgia*, a case where the Supreme Court had granted constitutional protection to the private possession of obscene materials. The *Stanley* Court had held that "the right to receive information and ideas, regardless of their social worth, . . . is fundamental to our free society,"[62] and had asserted a "right to satisfy [one's] intellectual and emotional needs in the privacy of [one's] own home."[63] For obvious reasons NORML argued that the private possession/use of marijuana deserved no less protection than obscene materials, but Circuit Judge Tamm responded:

"NORML tries to bootstrap the Stanley right of privacy in the home into a fundamental right that protects all

---

[61] At the time, other scholars also noted the NORML court's backwards approach. As Brashear observed: "the opinions suggest that the courts were influenced more by the absence of an express amendment protecting marijuana use than by the inapplicability of the right of privacy." Brashear, *Marijuana Prohibition and the Constitutional Right of Privacy* (1975) 581

[62] *Stanley v. Georgia*, 394 U.S. at 564

[63] Id. at 565

activities taking place therein. This reading reverses the proper analysis. The home offers refuge for activities grounded in other protected rights. The right protected in Stanley was the first amendment right to read and receive information even if the information itself was not constitutionally protected. Without that first amendment right at issue, Stanley would have no right to privacy in the home."[64]

Again, we see the same backwards reasoning in effect. If the founders' conception of rights is brought to bear it is Judge Tamm that "reverses the proper analysis," as the home *does not* merely "offer refuge for activities grounded in other protected rights." Instead, it offers refuge for *activities grounded in the principles from which other constitutionally protected rights are derived*. These are the principles of fundamental justice, principles such as those of dignity, autonomy, proportionality, equality, non-arbitrariness, limited government, and the liberty presumption. They are all connected and while unenumerated, they are the principles that breathe life and substance into the enumerated rights.

2.2.1. Flawed Natural Rights Analysis

Apropos first principles, we must address the courts' natural rights reasoning, which mirrors the same mistaken thinking. In *Seeley*, the plaintiff asserted that the legislature's placement of marijuana in schedule I of controlled substances violated article I, § 32 of the Washington Constitution, which provides "[a] frequent recurrence to fundamental principles

---

[64] *NORML v. Bell*, 488 F. Supp. 123 (D.D.C. 1980)

is essential to the security of individual right and the perpetuity of free government." In this case, Ralph Seeley, a man diagnosed with a rare form of bone cancer (as well as being an able lawyer), argued that the phrase "frequent recurrence to fundamental principles" suggested that the framers retained the notion that natural rights should be considered when protecting individual rights. Defending himself, he claimed that this section of the Washington Constitution designated "extra-constitutional fundamental principles as essential to the security of individual rights," and that it was evidence of the framers' belief in natural law. He brought forth evidence that the notion of fundamental principles was central to natural law theories at the time the Constitution was adopted and that by adopting art. I, § 32 the framers intended to expand the scope of individual rights protected by the Constitution. On this basis, he held that the Constitution granted him a right to have marijuana prescribed as medical treatment for the nausea and vomiting associated with chemotherapy.

The courts' analysis is worth noting, as it is another testimony to the intellectual barrenness of unprincipled reasoning. As discussed in part two, the Constitution was a natural rights document, one by which the founders positivized the higher, unwritten natural law. The "frequent recurrence" Clause was an offshoot of this thinking and it was to be a reminder from the founders of the importance of anchoring the body of law to first principles. They knew that powerful forces would conspire to deprive the people of their government and that a system of arbitrary law was how this would be done. Thus, the purpose of this section of the Washington Constitution was to guard against the influence of these forces and the despotic system of law that would be their crowning achievement.

As seen from a principled perspective, this is the only sensible interpretation of the "frequent recurrence" Clause. Just like the Ninth Amendment, it clearly means what it says, and its purpose was to ensure that the relationship between the individual and state would be constantly recalibrated into one of harmony with first principles.

Just like the Ninth Amendment, however, this Clause would prove difficult for most judges to come to terms with, and as soon as a system of arbitrary law was in place they would join ranks to protect it. We have already seen why. Because they fail to see the bigger picture, it is their nature to support the status quo—and because they also have an authoritarian bent, this status quo will favor the agents of tyranny rather than liberty. It goes without saying that, to these people, the very idea of a return to first principles will be anathema. One way or another it must be discouraged, and whether it be for reasons of ignorance or political expediency, this is what most jurists have done.

Hence, it should come as no surprise that the Washington Court chose this route. As if they were interpreting ancient hieroglyphs whose meaning was long since lost, the justices made no real effort to decipher the true meaning of the "frequent recurrence to fundamental principles" Clause. Instead, the majority simply noted that it had been used infrequently by the judiciary and that Washington jurisprudence had yet to see a consistent approach to this clause. From there on, following their authoritarian proclivity, they jumped to the conclusion that the framers must have intended to leave it to the government to legislate as it saw fit. And to support this thesis, so out of step with the founders' temperament, they laid bare an equally blemished understanding of natural law. As the majority put it: "Respondent fails to identify a natural right, in existence at the time of the constitution's adoption, to use marijuana or to choose a particular medical treatment." And because "[n]either constitutional history [n]or pre-existing state law indicate that using marijuana is a right that the Washington Constitution was designed to protect," the court deduced that "art. I, § 32 was not meant to provide a substantive right to use marijuana for medical treatment."[65]

Again, we are provided with an extraordinary example of the cognitive despondency that defines arbitrary law. For one, the court's decision smacks of insincerity and bias. Humans have for tens of thousands of years used different substances to experience different states of consciousness[66] and only the last hundred years have we had laws restricting the use of some of these substances. As pertains to the medical use of marijuana, which was the court's inquiry, it has been used in Asian and Middle Eastern countries for at least 2,600 years for these purposes. It first appeared in Western medicine in 60 A.D. in the pharmacopoeia of Dioscorides and it has been listed in subsequent pharmacopoeias since that time. In the 19th century, marijuana was widely used for a variety of ailments, including muscle spasms, and cannabis was still to be found in the British Pharmaceutical Codex as late as 1949. While the *Seeley* court didn't mention any of this, other courts

---

[65] *Seeley v. State*, 132 Wash. 2d 776, 940 P.2d 604 (1997) 622

[66] "The use of psychoactive plants or fungi to alter consciousness is probably a nearly universal human cultural activity. Ethological evidence of the consumption of psychoactive plants among a variety of animal species, as well as archaeological evidence of early human substance use, suggests that the roots of such practices are a longstanding part of the cultural history of humanity and cannot be reduced to some degenerate or delinquent modern phenomenon." Tupper & Labate, *Plants, Psychoactive Substances and the International Narcotics Control Board* (2012) 18

have recognized the historical use of marijuana for medicinal purposes, and as the Ninth Circuit held in *Raich v. Gonzales*, "[i]t is beyond dispute that marijuana has a long history of use—medically and otherwise—in this country."[67] As the *Raich* court recognized, it was only with the passage of the Controlled Substances Act in 1970 that Congress placed marijuana on Schedule I, taking it outside of the realm of all uses, including medical, under federal law.

In the history of man, then, it was not until the 20th century that the right to self-medicate was no longer taken for granted, and so it is difficult to see how the Washington Court earnestly could have believed that there was no "natural right, in existence at the time of the constitution's adoption, to use marijuana or to choose a particular medical treatment." The right to self-medicate was at this time incontestable, and the court's opinion is made even more suspect by the fact that this right is a subset of an (if possible) even more fundamental right, the right to bodily integrity. This right has deep roots in American history and legal tradition. There is a wealth of jurisprudence to draw upon, and it is indisputable that the right to be free of government intrusion with respect to one's body has roots in natural rights principles and the philosophy of individual autonomy. American legal precedent has consistently upheld legal protection for this individual right, and even before the Founding it was a firmly established basis of Anglo-American law.[68]

---

[67] *Raich v. Gonzales, et al.*, 500 F.3d. 864 (9th Cir. 2007)

[68] Blackstone recognized a right to personal security that "consists in a person's legal and uninterrupted enjoyment of his life, his limbs, his body, his health, and his reputation." He extended protection to the "preservation of a man's health from such practices as may prejudice or annoy it." 1 BLACKSTONE, *COMMENTARIES* 128, 133 (1765)

Aside from the denial of historical evidence, the court's claim that the applicant "fails to identify a natural right, in existence at the time of the constitution's adoption, to use marijuana or to choose a particular medical treatment," indicates that the justices either (1) knew nothing of the founders' natural law reasoning or (2) willfully ignored it. It suggests that they were looking for a textual source explicitly stating that "We, the framers of the U.S. Constitution, hold marijuana use to be a natural right," when in fact the framers could be counted upon to do no such thing. First of all, they saw no need to enumerate natural rights as their existence had nothing to do with textual basis. We have already seen that there is a written *and an unwritten* constitution of the United States. The former draws its legitimacy from the latter, and as the natural law belongs to the realm of unwritten law, the court's attack makes no sense. It might as well deny a right to have children, to wear a hat, to farm lands, or to go to sleep because the founders did not explicitly articulate these natural rights.[69]

Furthermore, in 1889, at the time of the adoption of the Washington Constitution, cannabis was a freely sold and frequently used medicine[70] and the framers could not see any reason for stating the obvious—that it was a natural right. Unlike modern day justices, they abided by a presumption of liberty, and unless marijuana use somehow violated the rights of others to live free and productive lives, there was no

---

[69] Considering that the Eighth Circuit, in *U.S. v. White Plume*, denied farming status as a protected right, the irony is complete. As it stands the state can now deny people a right to live off their land without offering a reasonable (much less compelling) justification.

[70] In the period between 1840 and 1900 more than 100 articles about the therapeutic value of cannabis were published in Europe and North America. See MATHRE, CANNABIS IN MEDICAL PRACTICE (1997)

question in their mind that it was a natural right. When it comes to this, Seeley's right to use marijuana for palliative relief from terminal illness can hardly be said to violate the rights of non-users to administer their own affairs as they see fit. And as Seeley's medicinal choice is "theoretically and practically consistent with the exercise of the fundamental rights of others," it is plainly "inferable from the axioms of natural law theory."[71]

Thus, Seeley's claim was firmly grounded in the principles of natural law. One does not have to look further than across the border to find a Supreme Court decision declaring it to be so,[72] and as Rufus King put it, "If people have no freedom to make such choices as cannabis over nicotine for their preferred lung irritant, what did the Constitution leave them?"[73]

2.3. Ignoring the Bigger-Picture Implications

We would do well to ponder King's question, for as seen from the principled perspective drug prohibition does implicate important rights. As seen from this perspective, the War on Drugs is an authoritarian attempt to control consciousness and it is not so much a war on drugs as a war on autonomous choice. As Graham Hancock noted, the fundamental premise of this war effort is that "we as adults do not have the right or

---

[71] Sweet & Harris, *Moral and Constitutional Considerations in Support of the Decriminalization of Drugs*, in FISH (ED.), *HOW TO LEGALIZE DRUGS* (1998) 455

[72] In *Regina v. Smith*, 2015 SCC 34, the Canadian Supreme Court held that Canadians have a fundamental right to use medical marijuana and that this liberty includes taking THC in whatever form the patient chooses.

[73] KING, *THE DRUG HANG UP* (1972) chapter 30

maturity to make sovereign decisions about our own consciousness and about the states of consciousness we wish to explore and embrace. This extraordinary imposition on adult cognitive liberty is justified by the idea that our brain activity, disturbed by drugs, will adversely impact our behavior toward others. Yet anyone who pauses to think seriously for even a moment must realize that we already have adequate laws that govern adverse behavior toward others and that the real purpose of the 'war on drugs' must therefore be to bear down on consciousness itself."[74]

The fact that is so obvious from the principled perspective, that the right to drugs is a right to control one's consciousness, the most intimate, elemental, and personal there is, has been lost on most individuals. This, most likely, is because they are born into a world where prohibitionist propaganda has defined the policy debate for nearly a century. And because they have been raised to believe in the one-sided and often untruthful image of drugs as a source of all our problems, they have fallen victim to an exaggerated enemy image. To them, therefore, drugs are simply bad. They are an evil to be eradicated by whatever means necessary, and only to the extent that this is done can our children be safe.

We shall have more to say on the enemy image of drugs and how it fails to mirror reality. However, leaving aside the question of whether drugs are "bad," it is undeniable that the point of taking drugs is to alter the chemical balance of the brain, leading to changes in a person's cognitive process— and it follows that fundamental rights necessarily are involved. As Professor Richards noted "the right of drug use, if it is a right, is a right associated with the control of

---

[74] HANCOCK (ED.), *THE DIVINE SPARK* (2015) 30-31

consciousness, and thus with the right of conscience itself, and should be understood accordingly."[75]

The U.S. Supreme Court has already recognized that "the right to receive information and ideas, regardless of their social worth, . . . is fundamental to our free society,"[76] and that, except in very limited cases, the right to be free from unwanted government intrusion in one's privacy is fundamental. The Court has also acknowledged that "the State may not, consistently with the spirit of the First Amendment, contract the spectrum of available knowledge,"[77] and that the "right to receive" recognized in *Stanley* is "a right to a protective zone ensuring the freedom of a man's inner life, be it rich or sordid."[78] Furthermore, the Court has acknowledged that people have a fundamental right to make certain "intimate and personal choices,"[79] and that "[a]t the heart of liberty is the right to define one's own concept of existence, of meaning, of the universe, and of the mystery of human life."[80] The Court has also noted that "[b]eliefs about these matters could not define the attributes of personhood were they formed under compulsion of the State,"[81] and that the First Amendment secures a "right of the individual to be free from governmental programs of thought control, however such programs might be justified in terms of permissible state objectives."[82]

---

[75] RICHARDS, *TOLERATION AND THE CONSTITUTION* (1989) 281

[76] *Stanley v. Georgia*, 394 U.S. 557 (1969) 564

[77] *Griswold*, 381 U.S. 479 (1965)

[78] *United States v. Reidel*, 402 U.S. 351 (1971) 360 (Harlan J., concurring)

[79] *Casey*, 505 U.S., at 851

[80] Id. at 851

[81] Id.

[82] *Reidel*, 402 U.S. 351 (1971) 359 (Harlan J., concurring)

All this applies to the drug law, for the War on Drugs is nothing if not an attempt to control our thought processes. It may be for our own good or for the good of society; this is a question that remains to be addressed, and it can only be properly addressed under the auspices of an independent, impartial, and competent tribunal. However, our thought processes are, at the deepest level, *what we are*, and as Hancock noted, "to the extent that we are not sovereign over our own consciousness, then we cannot in any meaningful sense be sovereign over anything else either."[83]

Also, as seen from the principled perspective, drug use implicates another important right—the right to liberty. Because the state uses the criminal law to address the "problem" of drug use, drug law violators, if caught, will be subjected to arrest and imprisonment. As documented in *To Right a Wrong*, scholars capable of principled reasoning insist that these people "have every right to demand a justification for how they have been treated,"[84] and that the criminal law therefore must be subject to unique scrutiny to ensure that no punishment is unjust. There is a rule of law that the more severe the sanction, the greater will be the burden of overcoming the liberty presumption. And as the drug law imprisons millions of people and threatens to imprison many millions more, it should be uncontroversial that the government must have very good reasons for doing so. This is the only way to honor the fundamental principles of law, and because liberty, as Professor Husak and other scholars have

---

[83] HANCOCK (ED.), *THE DIVINE SPARK* (2015) 3

[84] HUSAK, *OVERCRIMINALIZATION* (2008) 94-103

noted, "is a fundamental interest," it "should be subject to deprivation only by a compelling state interest."[85]

As the drug law clearly implicates autonomy and liberty rights, those justices capable of principled reasoning will insist that the government proves that this is the case. Judge Sweet, for instance, has argued forcefully that the right to drugs is a constitutionally protected autonomy right, and that "[b]ecause the right to self-determination is a fundamental right, any govern-mental action that encroaches upon it must be justifies by a 'substantial' state interest and be tailored in the narrowest manner possible."[86] As he continued: "governmental action encroaching on the right to self-determination faces a scale that is tipped heavily against it before the balancing analysis even begins,"[87] and pertaining

---

[85] Husak, *Two Rationales for Drug Policy*, in FISH (ED.), *HOW TO LEGALIZE DRUGS* (1998) 58. See also Colb, *Freedom from Incarceration* (1994) 812 ("The eighth amendment requires scrutiny of every form of punishment, with a concomitant determination of whether it is cruel and unusual. Substantive due process additionally requires strict scrutiny of every deprivation of a fundamental fight. Because incarceration involves both punishment and the deprivation of a funda-mental right, incarceration must accordingly withstand scrutiny under both the eighth amendment and the due process clause of the fourteenth (or fifth) amendment."); Materni, *The 100-plus Year old Case for a Minimalist Criminal Law* (2015) 27 ("when the government wants to regulate conduct through the most restrictive means at its disposal, and in such a way that the very core of liberty is affected, it needs to have a compelling interest to do so, coupled with the absence of less restrictive means to achieve that interest—in other words, criminal legislation should be subject to strict scrutiny.")

[86] Sweet & Harris, *Moral and Constitutional Considerations in Support of the Decriminalization of Drugs*, in FISH (ED.), *HOW TO LEGALIZE DRUGS* (1998) 483. To substantiate this claim, the authors refer to *United States v. O'Brien*, 391 U.S. 367, 377 (1968); *Young v. New York City Transit Authority*, 903 F.2d 146, 157 (2d Cir), cert. denied, 498 U.S. (1990); *Simon & Schuster, Inc. v. Members of New York State Crime Victims Bd.*, 112 S. Ct. 501, 514 (1991) (Kennedy J., concurring); *Loper v. New York City Police Department*, 802 F. Supp. 1029, 1041 (S.D.N.Y. 1992), aff'd, 999 F. 2d 699 (2d Cir. 1993)

[87] Ibid. 483

to the liberty encroachment other justices have also noted the need for strict scrutiny.[88]

2.3.1. How the Bigger-Picture Implications are Ignored

To most justices, however, none of this is obvious. As far as they are concerned drug use has no inherent value and neither does the freedom of the drug using population. Some will be more honest about admitting this than others. Nonetheless, their actions speak for themselves, for whenever challenges to the drug law are brought before the courts they will protect the law from critical review and drug users' autonomy and liberty rights will carry no weight in their analysis.

This is their modus operandi. To sustain the law, they must steer clear of the bigger picture and any coherent analysis. They must ignore the fundamental principles of justice, discount the factual picture, and narrow their focus to the point where their twisted and self-refuting logic is not too obvious. This is done by the following sleight-of-hand: They will define the right narrowly, look to precedent for guidance, and begin analysis with the supposition that the enumerated rights and a handful of others are the only worthy of protection. This approach to constitutional interpretation

---

[88] As Justice Levinson of the Hawaii Supreme Court held: "[a]ny criticism which attempts to deter courts from inquiring into the constitutionality of laws must distinguish between legislation which seeks to regulate economic and social relationships and that which intrudes into the purely private sphere of human life. In the former instance courts rightfully grant the legislature wide latitude for experimentation in the promotion of the general good. But, where the State endeavors to intrude into the individual's private life and regulate conduct having no public significance, it is the duty of the courts to offer a haven of refuge where the individual may secure vindication of his right to be let alone." *State v. Kantner*, 493 P.2d 306 (1972) 317-18 (Levinson J., dissenting)

obviously connects with their failure to understand the difference between shadow and light, but because of this backwards methodology challenges to the drug laws fail again and again. Medical marijuana challenges are put down because "the liberty interest specially protected by the Due Process Clause [does not] embrace a right to make a life-shaping decision on a physician's advice to use medical marijuana to preserve bodily integrity, avoid intolerable pain, and preserve life, when all other prescribed medications and remedies have failed."[89] Traffickers and distributors will be denied their right to a fair trial "[b]ecause there is no colorable claim of a fundamental constitutional right to import or to distribute marihuana."[90] And even hemp farmers will be denied their day in court, because "[t]he Supreme Court has not declared 'farming' to be a fundamental right."[91]

The reasoning is false on all accounts because the rule of narrowing blinds the justices to the real issue, which is the law's relation to the fundamental principles of justice. To know if there is a right to use cannabis for medical, recreational, or religious reasons; to know if there is a right to produce or distribute marijuana commercially; and to know if there is a right to grow hemp, the court must first look at this underlying issue—but this is never done. Because most judges are not capable of operating at a more abstract level of generality (i.e., in principled terrain), they will cling on to what little they can grasp and begin in the other end, with the few enumerated rights. These textual sources will be used to consider the issue, and because drug use, possession, production, distribution, etc., is not explicitly granted by the

---

[89] *Raich v. Gonzales, et al.*, 500 F.3d. 864 (9th Cir. 2007)

[90] *United States v. Bergdoll*, 412 F. Supp. 1308 (D. Del. 1976) 1313

[91] *United States v. White Plume*, 447 F.3d 1067 (2005)

Constitution, they will look to the unenumerated right to privacy to see if it can contain the asserted right in question.

Now, the only way this could be done with some sincerity would be *first* to formulate a general conception of the right to privacy and *then* determine whether the possession/use/ sale of cannabis was fit to be included. In the history of the drug laws, however, only one court has ever done so. This was the *Ravin* court, and it found it impossible to formulate a general idea of privacy which did not include drug use. In its general outline of privacy, it was defined as "a right of personal autonomy in relation to choices affecting an individual's personal life" and "a right to be let alone." From this characterization it followed quite naturally that the use of cannabis in the privacy of one's home had to be included in such a right, and this is what the court confirmed.

Perhaps for this reason no other courts have followed the *Ravin* court's example. Instead, they will skip this part and go directly to the fundamental rights test already discussed; they will ask if cannabis use is of such importance that it is "implicit in the concept of ordered liberty," and as this test is flexible enough to accommodate any bias, no court has found drug use deserving of constitutional protection.

When it comes to this, we have already seen that the fundamental rights analysis, the rule of narrowing, and the presumption of constitutionality are not only interconnected and symptomatic of the justices' closed mindset. As we have seen they are also unconstitutional, for while the presumption of liberty and the equal treatment of all rights claims are inferable from first principles, these doctrines are not. In truth, they are merely helpful means of divesting with proper thinking and frowned upon constitutional challenges, and nowhere is this better seen than in drug cases. By narrowing their focus most justices somehow manage to escape the inevitable conclusion that autonomy and liberty rights are important rights worthy of strict scrutiny. This can only be achieved by applying a frame of reference so detached from reality that it becomes possible to ignore the logic that dictates otherwise; that the rights at issue are not only about a right to bodily integrity and to control our own thought processes, but a right also not to be imprisoned for doing so—rights that must be called fundamental if the word is to have any meaning at all.[92]

It is also interesting to note that in the current state of affairs, the game is always rigged in favor of the state. As pertains to the rule of narrowing, therefore, it is no coincidence that constitutional challenges must be defined at its most specific level, whereas this rule is not applied to the state. The courts, for instance, do not demand that the state justifies its aggression by narrowing down the issue as to whether "a state has a right to persecute and imprison non-violent citizens for exercising their autonomy rights in ways that directly hurt no one." They do not insist that the state justifies its assault on liberty by narrowing down the issue as to whether "a state has a right to harass and incarcerate individuals for trying to experience their connection to God more directly in ways that truthfully harm no one." And they do not ask the state to justify its violent onslaught against citizens by narrowing down the issue as to whether "it has a right to hunt down and lock away individuals for striving towards greater levels of well-being and happiness in ways

---

[92] As Tribe dryly noted, "I would suppose that protecting your ability to control your own body would have to be on anyone's short list of basic liberties or privileges and immunities in our system of government." Tribe, *On Reading the Constitution* (1986) 63

that directly affect no one—not even themselves—negatively."

At least 90 percent of all drug use conforms to these criteria and yet the courts would never think to ask the state to defend its hostility to autonomous choice in this way. True to their authoritarian inclination, the justices would never even consider looking for exactly where in the Constitution such a right could be granted to the state. Instead, it is the individual that must vindicate his choice of drugs and every conceivable doubt benefits the state. The presumption of liberty being effectively reversed, what we are dealing with is, of course, a presumption of guilt, and so it is that the American system does sneakily what fascist jurists did openly.[93]

To summarize, this is the problem with current doctrines. Aside from being unconstitutional, they are the result of the isolated, fragmented, and freedom-fearing perspective that defines arbitrary law, and it comes as no surprise that they are well tailored to help the justices ignore the bigger-picture implications. The courts' restricted focus effectively defines away the right we want to validate, as the judge is free to draw upon his personal bias to conclude that drug use is not important enough to merit protection. Never mind that many people and religious groups attest to the ability of some drugs to communicate with the Divine;[94] never mind that some of these drugs have been used by wisdom seekers for millennia; never mind that some of them have a proven record for

---

[93] To quote Vincenzo Manzini, a leading jurist in Mussolini's Italy: "nothing more incongruous and paradoxical can be imagined than the presumption of innocence . . . if a presumption indeed needs be, that should be a presumption of guilt." Materni, *The 100-plus Year old Case for a Minimalist Criminal Law* (2015) 22

[94] See *infra* notes 95, 117, 169

facilitating physical and psychological healing;[95] never mind that they are important tools for personal growth; never mind that most drug use is personally rewarding and socially unproblematic;[96] never mind that people with a history of moderate drug use on average are better functioning than non-drug users;[97] never mind that there is evidence to suggest that drug use *enhances* self-control and autonomy, whereas prohibition undermines conditions of autonomy;[98] never mind that 1.5 million Americans are arrested every year for violating this law; never mind that their use doesn't directly harm anyone else; never mind that prohibition has failed to reduce the supply and demand of drugs;[99] never mind that

---

[95] Clinical research on psychedelic drugs has yielded positive results in the following areas: Criminal recidivism, relationship counseling, treatment of substance abuse and addiction, PTSD, depression, end-stage psychotherapy with the dying, and obsessive-compulsive disorder, as well as being unique tools for stimulation of the meditative state and elicitation of mystical experience. See WINKELMAN & ROBERTS (EDS.), *PSYCHEDELIC MEDICINE* (2007); Grob, et al., *Pilot Study of Psilocybin Treatment for Anxiety in Patients with Advanced-stage Cancer* (2011) 71-78; Mash, *Ibogaine Therapy for Substance Abuse Disorders* in BRIZER & CASTANEDA (EDS.), *CLINICAL ADDICTION PSYCHIATRY* (2010) 50-60; Vollenweider & Kometer, *The Neurobiology of Psychedelic Drugs: Implications for the Treatment of Mood Disorders* (2010) 642-651. Anthropologists generally agree that the use of these psychedelic drugs is beneficial to the cultures that use them. See Ibid and SZASZ, *CEREMONIAL CHEMISTRY* (2003) 126. See also notes 117, 169

[96] Scholars have pointed out that drug use is a natural part of life, an important aide to the full development of individual potential. See DUKE & CROSS, *AMERICA'S LONGEST WAR* (1993) 153-54; WISOTSKY, *BEYOND THE WAR ON DRUGS* (1990) 201-02; MILLER, *THE CASE FOR LEGALIZING DRUGS* (1991) 152-57; MILLER, *DRUG WARRIORS AND THEIR PREY* (1996) 1-7

[97] Longitudinal studies of drug users indicate that adults who once had been moderate drug users are presently "the psychologically healthiest subjects, healthier than either abstainers or frequent users." Compared to moderate users, abstainers "show some signs of relative maladjustment." Shedler & Block, *Adolescent Drug Use and Psychological Health: A Longitudinal Inquiry* (1990) 612, 625

[98] Husak, *Liberal Neutrality, Autonomy, and Drug Prohibitions* (2000) 69-70

[99] This is well known. For example, *Analysis of Marijuana Policy* (June 1982) prepared by the National Research Council's Committee concluded that: "It can no longer be argued that use would be much more widespread and the problematic effects greater today if the policy of complete prohibition did not exist." 29-30

there are less invasive means of dealing with any social problems arising from their use; and never mind that the destructive consequences of prohibition are tearing the fabric of society apart.[100] None of this matter. In fact, it is consistently ignored because of the courts' narrow focus.

2.4. Reasoning from the Narrowed-Down Perspective

We have seen that there are autonomy and liberty interests at stake in challenges to the drug laws and there is more to say on how they are disparaged. We have already discussed how the rule of narrowing dissociates the right in question from the bigger picture, making it possible to ignore the bigger context and the fundamental issues at play. Furthermore, we can count on the courts to deny the plaintiff's rights claim any merit by (1) belittling the rights claim, (2) focusing on precedent and refusing to expand the area of protection, (3) misframing the issue, (4) relying on falsehoods and an exaggerated enemy image, (5) applying different kinds of logic to otherwise similar cases, (6) applying the same logic to otherwise dissimilar cases, and (7) emptying words of their essential meaning.

---

[100] To quote the UNDP: "evidence shows that in many countries, policies and related enforce-ment activities focused on reducing supply and demand have had little effect in eradicating production or problematic drug use. As various UN organizations have observed, these efforts have had harmful collateral consequences: creating a criminal black market; fuelling corruption, violence, and instability; threatening public health and safety; generating large-scale human rights abuses, including abusive and inhumane punishments; and discrimination and marginalization of people who use drugs, indigenous peoples, women, and youth." UNDP, *Perspectives on the Development Dimensions of Drug Control Policy* (2015) 2

2.4.1. Belittling the Rights Claim

This tactic takes many forms. The *NORML* court, for instance, in discussing if smoking marijuana was worthy of constitutional protection, concluded in the negative by comparing the use of cannabis to previously accepted activities. First, it took for granted that "the act of smoking does not involve the important values inherent in questions concerning marriage, procreation, or child rearing."[101] Then, referring to previous decisions where the courts had recognized the use of contraceptives as constitutionally protected, the court stated that "its use predominantly as a 'recreational drug' undercuts any argument that its use is as important as [such objectives]."[102] It bears noticing that FC scholars and justices have refuted this part of the argument.[103] Nevertheless, to support the validity of this

---

[101] *NORML*, 488 F.Supp. 133

[102] Id.

[103] Judge Sweet and Edward Harris comments on this part of the NORML court's analysis: "In its analysis the court not only dismisses the value of 'recreational' activity but actually counts the recreational aspect of the activity against the significance of the activity. In doing so, however, the court necessarily fails to grasp both the recreational aspect of nonprocreational sexual relations implicitly recognized in *Griswold* and the significance of the fundamental right to recreation that individuals have in their pursuit of life, liberty, and happiness." Sweet & Harris, *Moral and Constitutional Considerations in Support of the Decriminalization of Drugs*, in FISH (ED.), *HOW TO LEGALIZE DRUGS* (1998) 482. The Authors continue on this footnote: "The right to recreation is implied in the concepts of liberty and happiness set forth in the Declaration of Independence. In *Olff v. East Side Union High Sch. Dist.*, 404 U.S. 1042 (1972), Justice Douglas identifies recreation as a fundamental right implied in the concept of liberty: "The word 'liberty' is not defined in the Constitution. But, as we held in *Griswold v. Connecticut*, it includes at least the fundamental rights 'retained by the people' under the Ninth Amendment. One's hair style, like one's taste for food, or one's liking for certain kinds of music, art, reading, recreation, is certainly fundamental in our constitutional scheme—a scheme designed to keep government off the backs of people." (481)
Justice Levinson of the Hawaii Supreme Court had this to say on the constitutional right to privacy: "[It] encompasses more than just freedom from government surveillance. It guarantees to the individual the full measure of control over his own

conclusion, the court quoted the *Ravin* court's assumption that "few would believe they have been deprived of something of critical importance if deprived of marijuana."[104]

Just like the *Ravin* court, the *NORML* court provided no evidence that this was so. It merely took this for granted. However, perhaps this is not really true. After all, drug users will go through extraordinary difficulties to pursue their habits. Even though government agents have done everything in their power to make life a living hell for them, they have had no success in deterring drug use. Today, hundreds of millions of people around the world will risk the hassles of the criminal sanction to experience their preferred states of consciousness and drug use persists even in those countries where the death penalty is provided.

This being so, the eagerness with which we pursue a choice in drugs could be seen as a testimony to the legitimate interest in question. At the very least, scholars have pointed out that the judgment of individual drug users is far more reliable than that of the state,[105] and as Bakalar and Grinspoon noted:

> "If it ever became necessary for the government to use vast amounts of money and personnel to curb an organized illicit traffic in [some] other commodity forbidden by consumer protection laws, the law would

---

personality consistent with the security of himself and others. This freedom to choose one's own plan of life is essential to the pursuit of happiness and the enjoyment of life and thus finds additional protection in article I, section 2 of the Hawaii Constitution. In the instant case, the State's infringement upon this right of personal autonomy becomes apparent when one understands the nature of marihuana and the reasons for its use." *State v. Kantner*, 493 P.2d 306 (1972) at 315 (Levinson J., dissenting) (references omitted)

[104] *Ravin v. State*, 537 P.2d at 502

[105] DUKE & CROSS, *AMERICA'S LONGEST WAR* (1993) 152

probably be repealed. If people wanted the commodities so much, we might conclude that they have a legitimate interest and value strong enough to outweigh any argument for prohibition. In other words, we would handle the problem as we handle mountain climbing, hang-gliding, or motorcycle racing: We would treat it as a matter of preferred tastes and activities (however questionable) rather than consumer error."[106]

The *NORML* and the *Ravin* courts are not the only ones that have failed to add any importance to people's choice in drugs. Later courts have basically copied the *NORML* court's analysis,[107] and to this day they have all excepted drug use from those personal rights that can be deemed "fundamental" or "implicit in the concept of ordered liberty." To them, accepting drug use as a right to autonomy or privacy seems so contrary to the values upon which society is erected that even "obscene materials" have better protection. This is the case even though drugs have more potential to bring about new insights and mental discoveries of any real value, but this aspect of drug use has gone neglected.

The bias against drug use is so great that no court has attributed any weight to the positive aspects of drug use.[108] Even though most drug use is unproblematic to society and rewarding to the users, it is portrayed as an evil to be eradicated. Hence, autonomy and liberty rights are easily disparaged, for if drugs are "bad" what interest could be at

---

[106] BAKALAR & GRINSPOON, *DRUG CONTROL IN A FREE SOCIETY* (1998) 19

[107] E.g., *United States v. Maas*, 551 F. Supp. 645 (D.N.J. 1982) 647

[108] Some of the benefits of drug use are artistic creativity, spiritual enlightenment, and consciousness expansion. See WEIL, *THE NATURAL MIND* (1986); SHULGIN, *PIKHAL: A CHEMICAL LOVE STORY* (1992); STOLAROFF, *THANATOS TO EROS* (1994); notes 93, 167

stake in prohibition? If drug use is a menace to society, why should we not imprison the people who ensure its continuation? Why should we think twice about this?

To most judges, no further thinking is needed. However, they must find a way to deny drug users a fair trial, and this is how it is done.

2.4.2. Disparaging Autonomy Rights

When defending drug users' autonomy rights, many lawyers have argued the First Amendment. To reason with the courts this has been a traditional way forward, as the courts will consistently mistake text for principle, thinking the text to be the source of a right. Whether it be for reasons of ignorance or convenience, therefore, many lawyers have accepted this false premise and held that drug use comes under the protection of the First Amendment.

Leaving aside the fact that there is no need to anchor drug users' autonomy rights in the First Amendment to determine if drug use is a protected activity, their thinking is understandable. First, the courts expect the appellant to hang his rights-claim on one or more enumerated rights, and secondly, autonomy is recognized as being at the heart of the First Amendment.[109] Thus, as scholars of law and philosophy have noted that the concept of autonomy by necessity includes the right to choose which drugs are to be ingested,[110] one would

---

[109] Husak, *Two Rationales for Drug Policy*, in FISH (ED.), *HOW TO LEGALIZE DRUGS* (1998) 45-47

[110] Husak, *Liberal Neutrality, Autonomy, and Drug Prohibitions* (2000) 64 ("Feinberg for example, writes that 'the kernel of the idea of autonomy is the right to make choices and decisions—what to put into my body, what contacts with my body to permit, where and how to move my body through public space, how to use

think that the courts would be interested to see if this is in fact so.

After all, without a freedom to experience the whole range of thought, emotion, and sensation connected to the human experience, we are being deprived sources of insight. And as drug use *does* provide "new sources of belief and experience,"[111] it follows that it must be "protected under the first amendment because it supplies these necessary preconditions to speech and expression."[112] According to this reasoning, just as the Constitution treats restrictions upon speech, press, and religion as a substantial harm, so the judiciary should recognize that the Constitution applies the same protection for infringements on our freedom to think. It should recognize that our freedom to form opinions, to gain new perspectives, and to develop and exercise our thought processes *as we see fit* is not merely a prerequisite for constitutional protections, but that without it the avowed right to "life, liberty and the pursuit of happiness" becomes an Orwellian ruse.

As thought precedes verbal communication the freedom of speech would be meaningless without us first recognizing a fundamental right to cognitive liberty. Recognizing this right is equally central to our freedom of religion: without an absolute freedom to connect with our inner world by whatever means we deem fit, it would mean little more than

---

my chattels and physical property, what personal information to disclose to others, what information to conceal, and more.' Since drugs are 'put into [the] body,' drug use is unquestionably autonomous on this conception."); DUKE & CROSS, *AMERICA'S LONGEST WAR* (1993) 152; Michael Moore, *Liberty and Drugs*, in DE GREIFF (ED.), *DRUGS AND THE LIMITS OF LIBERALISM* (1999) 61-109

[111] Brashear, *Marijuana Prohibition and the Constitutional Right of Privacy* (1975) 581

[112] Ibid.

a freedom to accept established authority.[113] Provided therefore that the use of drugs can be shown to help us grasp new concepts, to access new ideas, to gain spiritual insight, and to rediscover and illuminate the majesty of our inner landscape, it follows that our right to use drugs, while enumerated, is an integral part of the Constitution. As Justice Brandeis described the founders' quest:

> "The makers of our Constitution undertook to secure conditions favorable to the pursuit of happiness. They recognized the significance of man's spiritual nature, of his feelings and of his intellect. They knew that only a part of the pain, pleasure and satisfactions of life are to be found in material things. They sought to protect Americans in their beliefs, their thoughts, their emotions and their sensations. They conferred, as against the Government, the right to be let alone—the most comprehensive of rights and the right most valued by civilized men."[114]

The fact that drug use should be included in the right to be let alone is obvious to those that reason from a principled perspective. Since the 1960s scholars have made the connection between drug use and the rights protected by the

---

[113] As Tribe and Dorf noted, "the freedom of speech, the freedom of religion, and so forth make sense only if connected by a broader and underlying principle of freedom of thought and conscience. . . . Free speech is an empty freedom if not possessed by a free mind." Tribe & Dorf, *Levels of Generality in the Definition of Rights* (1990) 1069 (referring to Justice Harlan's conception of liberty)

[114] *Olmstead v. United States*, 277 U.S. at 478 (1928) (Brandeis, J., dissenting)

First Amendment,[115] and Justice Levinson of the Hawaii Supreme Court recognized as much when he said that:

> "The individual who uses marihuana does so from choice, in the pursuit of various goals which may include the relief from tension, the heightening of perceptions, and the desire for personal and spiritual insights. In short, marihuana produces experiences affecting the thoughts, emotions and sensations of the user. These experiences being mental in nature are thus among the most personal and private experiences possible. For this reason I believe that the right to be let alone protects the individual in private conduct which is designed to affect these areas of his personality."[116]

As I have said, the question of whether there are good reasons for a prohibition is not being addressed here. Perhaps there is evidence that some drugs are so "bad" that we cannot be allowed to choose for ourselves if we want to use them; we do not know because the issue has never been seriously reviewed. Nonetheless, *they can* be used for these purposes,[117] and so First Amendment rights *are* implicated in drug use.

The reason why so many lawyers have tried to get the courts to accept the idea that drug users' autonomy is

---

[115] Dichter, *Marijuana and the Law* (1968) 862 ("Since the use of marijuana, even for the mere enjoyment of the experience, is a form of expression dealing solely with the mind, a strong argument can be made for bringing this extremely private form of expression within the ambit of the zone of privacy surrounding the freedom of expression.")

[116] *State v. Kantner*, 493 P.2d 306 (1972) 315 (Levinson J., dissenting)

[117] Certain drugs can be said to bring about states of mind in which new ideas and often profound information is attained. This is especially true of the psychedelic drugs—and this information can even be said to be of great importance to us as a society. See notes 95, 117, 169

protected by the First Amendment is that, if this is so, the state must show a compelling interest in denying drugs. The burden of evidence befalls prohibitionists, for as the U.S. Supreme Court once held, all rights must be construed liberally[118] and "[a] State's interest must be 'compelling' or 'paramount' to justify even an indirect burden on First Amendment rights."[119]

2.4.2.1. Denying the Principled Perspective

Now, this connection between drug use and the First Amendment, while compelling to those who reason from the bigger perspective, have not persuaded those who remain too entrenched in personal bias and cultural prejudice to connect with first principles. They must find a way to ensure that the drug law escapes scrutiny, and so, where the religious use of drugs is not at issue,[120] the courts will deny that First

---

[118] "It has been repeatedly decided that these Amendments should receive a liberal construction, so as to prevent stealthy encroachment upon or 'gradual depreciation' of the rights secured by them, by imperceptible practice of courts or by well-intentioned but mistakenly over-zealous executive officers." *Gouled v. United States*, 255 U.S. 304

[119] *Brazenburg v. Hayes et al.*, 408 U.S. 665 (1972); see also *Griswold* 381 U.S at 497 (Goldberg J., concurring) ("Where there is a significant encroachment upon personal liberty, the State may prevail only upon showing a subordinating interest which is compelling.")

[120] In those cases where appellants claim a right to use drugs on religious grounds the courts will accept that First Amendment rights are involved. However, except for a few cases regarding indigenous tribes' shamanic use of psychedelic drugs, (e.g., *People v. Woody*, 1964) courts will reject the appeal for strict scrutiny. In essence, they will simply assume that the appellants' claims are not sincere, and that even if they are, the requirements for a compelling interest are fulfilled if the legislature believes it has a compelling interest in prohibiting these drugs. See *Leary v. United States*, 383 F.2d 851 (1967); *United States v. Kuch*, 288 F. Supp. 439 (1968); *Gaskin v. State*, 490 S.W.2d 521 (1973); *United States v. Middleton*, 690 F.2d 820 (1982). For a fuller discussion of the issue, see Finer, *Psychedelics and Religious Freedom* (1968); Comment, *Free Exercise: Religion Goes to "Pot"* (1968); Doss & Doss, *On*

Amendment rights are involved. As one may expect, they have never cared to bolster their position by countering the argument above or by offering any convincing analysis in support of their thesis. All they have done is refer to the *Stanley* Court, where the justices, after holding that the possession of obscene materials was protected because the First Amendment right to receive information was involved, continued to say that:

> "What we have said in no way infringes upon the power of the State or Federal Government to make possession of other items, such as narcotics, firearms, or stolen goods, a crime. Our holding in the present case turns upon the Georgia statute's infringement of fundamental liberties protected by the First and Fourteenth Amendments. No First Amendment rights are involved in most statutes making mere possession criminal."[121]

On this basis the courts have denied that First Amendment rights are implicated in drug use. A proper constitutional interpretation, however, leaves us with another conclusion, for while the principles of justice "in no way infringes upon the power of the State or Federal Government to make possession of other items such as narcotics, firearms, or stolen goods, a crime," they do demand that no such activity can be made a crime unless the proposed legislation passes a proper balancing test—one that, as natural rights theorists would put it, can separate license from liberty. Such a test weighs the individual's autonomy and liberty interests

---

Morals, Privacy, and the Constitution (1971); Mazur, *Marijuana as a Holy Sacrament* (1991); Tupper & Labate, *Plants, Psychoactive Substances and the International Narcotics Control Board* (2012)

[121] *Stanley*, 394 U.S. at 568 (footnote 11)

against society's need for protection, and the extent to which the scales are tipped in favor of the individual depends on the facts. In this regard, criminalizing the possession of stolen goods will pass with flying colors whereas the criminalization of narcotics possession is less likely to succeed.

Whether we ground drug users' autonomy rights in the First or the Ninth Amendment is irrelevant. In either case, weighty individual interests are involved, and as the Supreme Court traditionally has reserved its heightened scrutiny for "values grounded in equality and personal autonomy,"[122] the state must show that even weightier considerations speak in favor of denying people a choice in drugs.

From a principled perspective, this is uncontestable. And unless the state can show that the drug law survives a proper analysis, the *Stanley* Court's oft-cited quote on the protection of privacy, properly modified, should read: "If the First Amendment means anything, it means that a State has no business telling a man . . . what books he may read, what films he may watch, *or what drugs he may take*. Our whole constitutional heritage rebels at the thought of giving government the power to control men's minds."[123]

---

[122] Bilionis, *The New Scrutiny* (2002) 103. Professor Bilionis referred to these cases: "See, e.g., *Cleburne*, 473 U.S. at 440 (noting that laws that classify by 'race, alienage, or national origin . . . are subjected to strict scrutiny and will be sustained only if they are suitably tailored to serve a compelling state interest,' that '[s]imilar oversight by the courts is due when state laws impinge on personal rights protected by the Constitution,' and that '[l]egislative classifications based on gender also call for a heightened standard of review'); *Carey v. Population Servs. Int'l*, 431 U.S. 678, 684-86 (1977) (espousing strict scrutiny for intrusions upon fundamental privacy rights as a matter of substantive due process); *Craig v. Boren*, 429 U.S. 190, 218 (1976) (espousing intermediate scrutiny under the Equal Protection Clause for laws that classify on the basis of sex); *Harper v. Va. State Bd. of Elections*, 383 U.S. 663, 669-70 (1966) (espousing strict scrutiny under the Equal Protection Clause for discriminatory infringements of fundamental interests); *McLaughlin v. Florida*, 379 U.S. 184, 192-93 (1964) (espousing strict scrutiny under the Equal Protection Clause for laws that classify on the basis of race)."

[123] *Stanley*, 394 U.S. at 565

2.4.3. Disparaging Liberty Rights

As seen, the courts have consistently refused to recognize drug users' autonomy rights and their liberty rights have not fared much better. The fact that many millions have been imprisoned because of the drug law and that the freedoms of millions more is at risk has never prompted the court to demand a justification.[124] In fact, in the American system of law, the freedom of drug users have no value, and economic regulations are more carefully scrutinized. As Judge Spiegel of the *Leis* court held:

> "We do not agree with the defendants that the Legislature is bound to adopt the 'least restrictive alternative' that would fulfill its purpose of protecting the health, safety and welfare of the community. The least restrictive alternative doctrine does not apply to the instant case. It has been limited to regulations affecting interstate commerce, constitutionally sheltered activity, and economic regulations. The Narcotic Drugs Law is not an economic regulation. It affects neither interstate commerce nor constitutionally sheltered activity."[125]

Also in *Schmitt*, the Michigan Court of Appeals attested to the perceived unimportance of drug users' liberty rights.[126] The defendant argued that, instead of the rational basis test, the court should use the substantial-relation-to-the-object test

---

[124] In *Ravin* and a few cases concerning the religious use of peyote and ayahuasca the state has had to defend its policy (and lost), but none of them focused on the liberty interest of drug users.

[125] *Commonwealth v. Leis*, 355 Mass. 189 (1969) 195-96 (references omitted)

[126] *People v. Schmidt, 86 Mich. App. 574 (1978)*

used in *Manistee Bank & Trust Co v. McGowan*.[127] In that case petitioner claimed a decision by the legislature to carve out a discrete exception to a general rule (such as requiring a showing of gross negligence by a guest passenger to recover for loss or injury from his host while all others recover on a showing of mere negligence) was unconstitutional. One would be hard pressed to argue that the liberty rights of 40 million Americans should count for less than the financial interests of a few people, but that did not discourage the Michigan court. As it said: "We do not find defendant's arguments on these points persuasive. The legislative decision to place controls on marijuana, from among the galaxy of substances, does not compare with the legislative decision to single out guest passengers for special treatment in recovering for a loss resulting from an automobile accident."[128] That was it, and so the court decided that the rational basis test would do fine.

Now, not only are economic rights more important than drug users' liberty rights, but the courts provide enhanced protection for commercial speech. Hence, laws prohibiting the advertising of prices for prescription drugs[129] and laws restricting the advertising of liquor, tobacco, and other harmful products[130] also receive heightened scrutiny. Any such restriction on commercial speech will be subjected to the substantial interest test where the government must prove that it directly advances the government's objective and that it is no more extensive than necessary to achieve that purpose. All

---

[127] *Manistee Bank & Trust Co v. McGowan*, 394 Mich. 655; 232 N.W.2d 636 *(1975)*

[128] *86 Mich. App. at 578*

[129] *Pharm. Bd. v. Va. Consumer Council*, 425 U.S. 748 (1976)

[130] *Liquor mart, Inc. v. Rhode Island*, 517 U.S. 484 (1996); *Lorillard Tobacco Co. v. Reilly*, 533 US. 525 (2001)

this, while drug users are being imprisoned en masse for laws that we have reason to suspect would fail any type of meaningful scrutiny, and that the judiciary to has shielded from review.

When it comes to this, the *Pickard* court[131] provides us with an example of how drug law violators' liberty rights are disparaged. The defendants had argued that strict scrutiny should be applied because their fundamental right to liberty was at stake, and the court confirmed this by stating that "[e]very person has a fundamental right to liberty in the sense that the government may not punish him unless and until it proves his guilt beyond a reasonable doubt at a criminal trial conducted in accordance with the relevant constitutional guarantees."[132] As seen from the bigger perspective, the "relevant constitutional guarantees" means that no one shall ever be imprisoned for violating laws that do not conform to the criteria laid out by the fundamental principles of justice. The defendants, however, should have suspected that something was amiss when the judge continued: "But substantive due process requires a 'careful description of the asserted fundamental liberty interest.' Hence, the right asserted in this case cannot be the broad fundamental liberty interest defendants claim."[133]

According to Judge Mueller, a general right to freedom from imprisonment did not define the right in question. More specifically defined, the right in question was if *marijuana producers* had a right to freedom from imprisonment and this notion was easily dismissed by the court. In support of her ruling the judge referenced a series of court decisions holding

---

[131] *Pickard, et. al.*, No. 2:11-CR-0449-KJM (2015)

[132] Id. at 24

[133] Id.

that there was "no fundamental right" to use, import, sell, or possess marijuana in any context, and that was all it took to deny a proper hearing.

The lack of analysis betrays an eagerness not to reflect on the subject. Indeed, the lack of coherence is palpable to anyone who cares to think about things, so let us see how the court jumped from a true premise to a false conclusion.

First, the judge accepted the premise that all individuals enjoy a fundamental right to be free from undue confinement. The appellants having made this claim, the court could not simply deny that this is not so—especially after the prosecution, in its supplemental brief, had admitted that:

"Defendants enjoy a fundamental right to liberty, [but the statute] does not encroach on that liberty interest. The only way it could would be if there were a constitutional right to manufacture marijuana, which of course there is not. If there were a constitutional right to manufacture marijuana, then the government would have to concede that the statute encroaches on that right, and the statute could only be sustained via proof that the law was narrowly tailored in support of a compelling governmental interest (strict scrutiny)."[134]

Now, we have established beyond contention that a constitutional right to be free from undue liberty deprivation exists, and the right thing to do would be to apply strict scrutiny and see if the drug law violated drug users'/ producers' autonomy and liberty rights. A proper balancing test would have provided the answer to this question and the court could not, like the prosecution, simply take for granted

---

[134] *United States v. Schweder, et al.*, Supplemental Brief (May 21, 2014) 14

that the law was beyond reproach. Remember that the Constitution "is cut out of one cloth" and that its purpose is to protect the individual from all undue interference. The light of first principles shines in *all* directions and it is impossible to determine if marijuana production is a fundamental right before these principles have been applied.

When it comes to this, the light of first principles is all we need to establish that the state must have good reasons to punish the individual for exercising his liberty/autonomy rights. And as the state has enacted such punishment for violations of the drug law, the law *must survive* a balancing test, one that shows compelling reasons for criminalizing such conduct. This means that a restriction must either (1) be in place to protect the rights of others in their individual capacity or (2) to protect the rights of others in a communal capacity. There are certain minimum criteria that a law must comply with to be lawful, and to determine if the drug law fulfills these criteria it must be subjected to the test of reason. Unless this is so, the right to be free from undue incarceration is rendered meaningless, as the state will be free to throw coffee drinkers, sugar consumers, pizza eaters, football players, and anti-war activists in prison simply by prohibiting such activities.

We must never forget that these laws would pass the rational basis test. Only a more searching review like the Lawton, strict scrutiny, or the internationally recognized proportionality analysis would stop them dead. And if we accept the premise (which human rights law does) that for a system of law to have legitimacy, it must provide protection against wanton infringements on our autonomy/liberty rights, we must also concede that the legitimacy of the U.S. justice system depends on the extent to which it ensures that its criminal law survives these more demanding types of scrutiny.

The failure of the *Pickard* court, then, becomes plain to see. For by accepting the doctrine that fundamental liberty interests must be narrowly defined and quoting previous court decisions that have held the use of cannabis not to be a fundamental right, the court quashed any meaningful application of the appellants' unalienable rights. It simply makes no sense to accept the premise that one has a fundamental right not to be unduly incarcerated and then use a rational basis test to see whether or not this fundamental right is violated—and yet this is what the court did.

Now some, like Judge Spiegel of the *Leis* court,[135] may say that drug law violators are not "unduly" incarcerated. They have, after all, chosen to exhibit behavior they know is prohibited. However, as Professor Colb points out, the fact that people can avoid punishment by conforming to the demands of a law does not "eliminate concerns about depriving an individual of a fundamental right when that deprivation is not necessary to serve a compelling governmental interest. . . . [E]ven people on notice of the consequences of their actions are entitled to a searching review of whether it is constitutionally appropriate to permit those consequences to follow."[136]

In challenges to the drug law therefore there are two issues before the court: (1) if drug use, production, distribution, etc., are constitutionally protected autonomy rights, and (2) if the incarceration of those who are engaged

---

[135] *Commonwealth v. Leis,* 355 Mass. 189 (1969) 199 ("The defendants are not charged with having a 'status' over which they have no control.")

[136] Colb, *Freedom from Incarceration* (1994) 796, 803

in these activities serves a compelling state interest.[137] None of these questions can be answered without bringing first principles into play and in both cases strict scrutiny must be applied. However, no matter what the court may decide as to the autonomy rights, it still must deal separately with the liberty rights at stake. It may, after all, be that some drugs are so harmful that the state can show a compelling interest in reducing their use, but even so the fourteenth and fifth amendment right to liberty from undue incarceration is a fundamentally protected right, putting constrains on how government may pursue an otherwise acceptable end.[138]

Because of this, all confinement must be justified according to the compelling interest test, and as Sherry Colb noted: "If incarceration is not necessary to a compelling interest, then the state does not confront the 'enemy' when it incarcerates the criminal; it confronts decent individuals and strips them of their most prized freedom—their liberty from confinement."[139]

---

[137] Already 40 years ago, professors of law pointed out the confusion on this issue, but the courts have neglected their duty to provide proper analysis. As Hindes stated in 1977: "Courts are not being asked to decide whether the Constitution implicitly says anything about smoking marijuana; they are being asked if there is any good reason for putting someone in jail for smoking marijuana. No principled evaluation of these cases can avoid reference to the broader social purpose of a criminal prosecution." Hindes, *Morality Enforcement Through the Criminal Law and the Modern Doctrine of Substantive Due Process* (1977) 381

[138] Colb, *Freedom from Incarceration* (1994) 812 ("The eighth amendment requires scrutiny of every form of punishment, with a concomitant determination of whether it is cruel and unusual. Substantive due process additionally requires strict scrutiny of every deprivation of a fundamental right. Because incarceration involves both punishment and the deprivation of a fundamental right, incarceration must accordingly withstand scrutiny under both the eighth amendment and the due process clause of the fourteenth (or fifth) amendment.")

[139] Ibid. 820

2.4.4. Denigrating Equal Protection Challenges

The tendency to belittle drug users' rights claims is seen in the courts' equal protection analysis. The Equal Protection Clause requires "that criminal statutory classification schemes cover all persons or things related to each other reasonably, logically or scientifically."[140] A criminal statute therefore violates equal protection if it treats similarly situated persons differently for reasons not rationally related to the purpose of the statute.[141]

Consequently, to the extent that we are dealing with the same supply and demand factors when it comes to licit and illicit drugs; to the extent that there are the same varying patterns of use associated with the different groups of drugs; and to the extent that comparisons of licit and illicit drugs indicate that there is no meaningful difference between those groups singled out for persecution and those we tolerate, there is evidence to suggest that the different categories of drugs lack a rational basis and that the illicit drug users are being denied the equal protection of the law. A fundamental premise of the social contract is that we all have a right to be treated with equal respect and concern. Hence, if the government has created two classes of drug users, it better have good reasons for using the criminal law against one group; and as always the burden is on the government to show a compelling interest in treating the two classes of people differently.

What this means is that the government must show that cannabis users, for instance, cannot enjoy the same liberty

---

[140] *State v. Kantner*, 493 P.2d 306 (1972) at 319 (Kobayashi, J., dissenting). See also *McLaughlin v. Florida*, 379 U.S. 184, 85 S. Ct. 283, 13 L. Ed. 2d 222 (1964); *Skinner v. Oklahoma*, 316 U.S. 535, 62 S. Ct. 1110, 86 L. Ed. 1655 (1942); *Lindsley v Natural Carbonic Gas Co*, 220 US 61; 55 L Ed 369; 31 S Ct 337 (1911)

[141] *Reed v. State*, 264 Ga. 466, 448 S.E.2d 189 (1994)

and autonomy rights as alcohol drinkers; that they for some reason represent a bigger social problem; that weighty social attentions necessitate that the criminal law be used against them; that the criminal law is an effective means to an end; that it is the least restrictive means available for dealing with the problems associated with cannabis use; and that the law reflects a proper balancing of the rights at stake. Because fundamental interests are involved, the law must be narrowly tailored to achieve its stated purpose. This means that both over- and under-inclusiveness is frowned upon, so let us see how the drug law conforms to these criteria.

2.4.4.1. Equality Analysis 101

As far as the Equal Protection Clause is concerned, assuming that the purpose of the drug law is to promote the general welfare, we can say that for the law to be a 100 percent reasonable application of the police power, two criteria must be met: (1) all those to whom the law applies must be morally blameworthy for acts against the public welfare, and (2) their transgressions must be more pronounced than the acts of individuals who are not singled out for persecution.

To the extent these criteria are fulfilled, the law can be said to treat similarly situated people the same. This is a prime tenet of the Equal Protection Clause but, looking closer, the classification does a poor job in this regard.[142] First of all, as the purpose of the law is to protect the public welfare, it can

---

[142] As Professor Husak noted: "The prior decision to prohibit some drugs while allowing others does not appear to reflect an impartial . . . judgment about their relative dangers. . . . This basis for distinguishing among various drugs poses a genuine threat to equal protection." Husak, *Two Rationales for Drug Policy* in FISH (ED.), *HOW TO LEGALIZE DRUGS* (1998) 43

only seriously concern itself with drug abuse—only drug abusers, to some extent, put the public welfare at risk. When the drug laws were enacted it was assumed that all drug use equaled abuse. However, there is evidence to presume that 90 percent of all drug consumers use drugs responsibly, that they are functional and well-behaved citizens, and that they represent no problem to the public welfare.[143]

If this is the case, the statute is overinclusive because it includes many people who have done nothing to deserve persecution. We should never forget that moral blame-worthiness is a primary criterion for subjecting people to the criminal law and that any degree of overinclusiveness is highly problematic.[144] In order for overinclusiveness to be legitimate, there must be extremely good reasons to maintain the classification. Only in circumstances of genuine emergency, where society is under threat by some imminent evil, can such measures be considered as acceptable.

Prohibitionists, for their part, believe that this is the case. They proceed upon the presumption that (1) drugs are a menace to society; (2) that their use has no intrinsic value; (3) that the threat is so profound that applying the criminal law is necessary for the protection of society; (4) that the law is effective in dealing with this threat; and (5) that less restrictive solutions would be unfit for purpose. In their mind, therefore, everything is as it should be. Even moderate prohibitionists believe drugs to be so bad that an over-

---

[143] The United Nations estimates that there are 250 million drug users worldwide, of which less than 10 percent are problem drug users. Report of the Global Commission on Drug Policy (June 2011) 13

[144] As Professors Tussman and tenBroek remind us, "such classifications fly squarely in the face of our traditional antipathy to assertions of mass guilt and guilt by association. Guilt, we believe, is individual, and to act otherwise is to deprive the individual of due process of law." Tussman & tenBroek, *The Equal Protection of the Laws* (1949) 352

inclusive law is justifiable. According to them, this collateral damage is the price society must pay for survival. More fanatical prohibitionists, however, insist that the law is not overinclusive at all. Because drugs are so dangerous, they will claim that *every* drug user is morally blameworthy for his or her choice in drugs; that even though they appear to be functional and well-behaved citizens they are a part of a greater problem; and that they deserve whatever punishment they get. As Daryl Gates, the chief of LAPD, once told Congress: "Casual drug users should be taken out and shot; we are at war and drug use is treason."[145]

Prohibitionists, of course, are entitled to their opinions. However, we are in a situation where we must accept on faith that such wartime measures are necessary, as these opinions have yet to be empirically confirmed.

Furthermore, the problematic nature of the drug law becomes even more apparent when we consider that not only is it overinclusive; it is also underinclusive as it fails to include substances that pose an even greater threat to the general welfare. When it comes to social harms, both alcohol drinkers and tobacco smokers represent a bigger threat to society.[146] And as professors Tussman and tenBroek noted: "Since the classification does not include all who are similarly situated with respect to the purpose of the law, there is a prima facie violation of the equal protection requirement of reasonable classification."[147]

To conclude, we find that the traits singled out are not synonymous with being offenses against the public welfare

---

[145] Gates testifying before the Senate Judiciary Committee 5. September 1990

[146] See DUKE & CROSS, *AMERICA'S LONGEST WAR* (1993) 22-77; WISOTSKY, *BEYOND THE WAR ON DRUGS* (1990) 185-215

[147] Tussman & tenBroek, *The Equal Protection of the Laws* (1949) 348

and that there are other, more obvious threats traits to society which are not singled out. On this basis, the law does a poor job at arresting offenders against the public welfare. It is both over- and underinclusive, and to sustain such classification on equal protection grounds the law "requires both the finding of sufficient emergency to justify the imposition of a burden upon a larger class than is believed tainted with the mischief, *and* the establishment of 'fair reasons' for failure to extend the operation of the law to a wider class of potential saboteurs."[148]

This is for the state to show. To this day it has never had to justify its actions on any other terms but its own. But when we recognize that 90 percent of those singled out have done nothing to harm the public welfare and that there are other population groups more deserving of reproach (if crimes against the common welfare is the criteria) it is difficult to escape the conclusion that the law arbitrarily singles out one class of citizens for persecution—and that the law, on Equal Protection terms, is unconstitutional.

It is also important to recognize that the people being persecuted are the least politically influential. We are in other words dealing with class-legislation because politicians have singled out a politically insignificant and marginal group for persecution while ignoring more powerful interest groups whose behavior puts the general welfare more at risk. Indeed, this is the sole defining trait for the criminalized group as a whole; people are persecuted not because they are threats to the public welfare, but because they are the scapegoats that must bear the brunt of the ingroup's prejudice and baseless intolerance.

---

[148] Ibid. 353

This is even openly admitted. As many prohibitionists are keen to point out, both alcohol and tobacco would be prohibited today, if these substances did not have a long history of use in Western society. In other times and places both alcohol and tobacco have been frowned upon (while some of the illicit drugs have been accepted) and it is well-known that culture, not reason, has been the defining characteristic of drug policy.[149] However, just as "culture" did not justify classifying people on grounds of race, gender, and certain sexual preferences, so it remains irrelevant for drug policy. The essence of the Equal Protection Clause is that people shall not be singled out for disadvantage or privilege based on morally irrelevant traits, and this is always the case when criminal punishment is involved. As Sunstein noted, "a difference is morally irrelevant if it has no relationship to individual entitlement or desert,"[150] and to sustain the criminalization of drug users the state must show that they are more deserving of punishment than alcohol drinkers.

There can be no doubt that the former is put at a systemic disadvantage. They live in a state of perpetual subordination without sufficient political power to defend themselves against policies enacted for reasons of prejudice or ill will. To this day they have been easy prey for politicians eager to find

---

[149] As the British Medical Association observed: "[A]lmost every psychoactive drug known to humanity, from alcohol to opium, has been regarded by some government and society as a dire threat to public order and moral standards, and by another government and another society as a source of harmless pleasure. Further, nations and governments sometimes change their views completely. Almost every society has at least one drug whose use is tolerated, while drugs used in other cultures are generally viewed quite differently and with deep suspicion. Mexican Indians may have disapproved of alcohol, but they used mescaline. Most Muslim cultures forbid alcohol, but they tolerate cannabis and opium." *Living with Risk: The British Medical Association Guide*, BMA Professional and Scientific Division (1987) 58

[150] Sunstein, *Homosexuality and the Constitution* (1994) 13

scapegoats and problem-areas to attack, and because the Equal Protection guarantee requires that "courts should protect those who can't protect themselves politically,"[151] drug users clearly deserve their day in court.

2.4.4.2. How the Equality Doctrine
Fails to Protect Drug Users

The equal protection standard discussed is a doctrine of principled law. It is, however, not the doctrine being applied in the United States, where a suspect classification doctrine has evolved under the auspices of the Supreme Court. Courts therefore will apply the equal protection standard described above only to legislation affecting a fundamental interest or laws targeting individuals on the basis of race, alienage, national origin, or sex. Hence, because drug use is not accepted as a fundamental right and the drug law makes no distinction relying on any of these categories, American justices will apply the rational basis standard. This means that they do not care if the law is a fit means to an end; they do not care if less invasive means could have been applied; and they do not care if there are no good reasons for treating illicit drug users differently than alcohol drinkers. In the instance of the drug law neither overinclusiveness nor under-inclusiveness is seen as a problem and the state is free to deal with the illicit drug users as it deems fit. As Justice Coler of the South Dakota Supreme Court held:

---

[151] Goldberg, *Equality Without Tiers* (2004) 553 (quoting Ely)

"Normally, the widest discretion is allowed the legislative judgment in determining whether to attack some, rather than all, of the manifestations of the evil aimed at; and normally that judgment is given the benefit of every conceivable circumstance which might suffice to characterize the classification as reasonable rather than arbitrary and invidious. . . . With specific reference to appellant's contention that marijuana is less harmful than tobacco and alcohol, we find support for our holding from the United States Court of Appeals, Second Circuit, which . . . concluded that 'If Congress decides to regulate or prohibit some harmful substances, it is not thereby constitutionally compelled to regulate or prohibit all. It may conclude that half a loaf is better than none.'"[152]

We shall have more to say on the courts' use of such words as "reasonable," "rational," and "arbitrary." Suffice now to say that they are void of meaningful content, as our politicians need only imagine that drug prohibition does some good and it does not matter if this is in fact so. As long as the drug law is "rational" to prohibitionists, the courts will defer to the legislature, and in this regard it is interesting to note the court's "half a loaf" comment. It is frequently used to deny drug users their day in court, but this abused quote stems from Thomas Jefferson and referred to the enumeration of rights in the Constitution. As discussed in *To Right a Wrong* there was a debate among the founders if rights should be enumerated in the Constitution. Many were against it because it would be impossible to enumerate every one, and as "it would be implying, in the strongest manner, that every right not included in the exception might be impaired by the

---

[152] *State v. Strong*, 245 N.W.2d 277 (1976) 279-80 (citations and quotation marks omitted)

government without usurpation . . . it would be not only useless, but dangerous, to enumerate" only some.[153] Jefferson, however, felt that the natural rights of the people were too easily infringed without a Bill of Rights, and despite the danger of an imperfect enumeration he held that "half a loaf is better than no bread. If we cannot secure all our rights, let us secure what we can."[154]

It is ironic that this passage, which initially attached to the liberty presumption, has become a tenet for arbitrary government. Orwellian judges have reversed Jefferson's intention; there are now no principled limits to the police power—and as it is employed to justify totalitarian notions, the transformation could not have been more profound.

While ironic, it is also symptomatic of the shift from the principled to arbitrary law. Following this reasoning, the Equal Protection Clause is rendered meaningless for all but a few fundamental rights and suspect classifications. It is stripped of its very essence, for could a law prohibiting doughnuts while exempting more harmful foods be valid? Would a law seeking to reduce motorcycle accidents be legitimate if it targeted only Harley Davidson motorcyclists? Could a law seeking to reduce the negative influence of videogames target only Nintendo users? Is it too much to ask that the state provides us with good reasons before targeting doughnut eaters, Harley Davidson motorcyclists, and Nintendo gamers for persecution?

---

[153] James Iredell quoted in Barnett, *The Ninth Amendment: It Means What It Says* (2006) 27-28

[154] Jefferson letter to Madison, March 15, 1789. Found in KURLAND & LERNER, *THE FOUNDERS' CONSTITUTION* (Web edition) Papers 14 at 659-61

As scholars and justices have pointed out, all these laws would pass the rational basis test,[155] and they have also noted the parallels between drug taking and such activities.[156] Hence, these examples are relevant. Not only are the drug laws unconstitutional for the exact same reasons, but the social burden associated with drug prohibition is worse than the evils that would result from these laws. As other food, motorcycle, and videogame manufacturers have products that can match the experience provided by the proscribed products, few would be likely to break the law to continue eating doughnuts, driving Harleys, or playing Nintendo. Consequently, the illicit economy following such criminalization would not even remotely trouble society to the extent that drug prohibition has done—and gangsters, paramilitary groups and secret services would not start wars to gain control of profits.

Yet this is the case with drug prohibition. Documenting the evils resulting from prohibition is beyond the scope of this book, but in Latin America 150.000 people die every year because of the drugs economy;[157] in America, roughly half of the 15.000 annual violent deaths can be attributed to drug prohibition;[158] and globally, 160.000 of the 200.000 drug-

---

[155] *State v. Mallan*, 86 Haw. 440, 950 P.2d 178 (1998) n. 67 (Levinson J., dissenting) (prohibition of the possession of peanuts would pass rational basis)

[156] "As an act of paternalism—protecting us from harming ourselves—drug prohibition is hard to distinguish from coercive governmental prohibition of obesity, excess television viewing, loafing, wasting money on unnecessary luxuries and infinite other ways in which people seem to act contrary to their long-term best interests. Even the nature of the self-harm is similar. The main cost of using drugs excessively is not poor health but an unrewarding life." DUKE & CROSS, *AMERICA'S LONGEST WAR* (1993) 151

[157] Organization of American States, *The Drug Problem in the Americas* (2013) 76

[158] "When I was a prosecutor, over half of the murders I prosecuted were 'drug law related' in the sense that the victim was killed as a result of a drug deal gone bad or a robbery of someone suspected of having either valuable drugs or money from

related deaths can be traced back to black-market factors.[159] It is impossible to ponder the trials posed by these factors. Caught between cops and gangsters, users exist between a rock and a hard place, even though substances like alcohol and tobacco are freely available. *This* is a testimony to the importance of their drugs of choice. *This* should tell us that their choice is not to be taken lightly, attributing to it no value or benefit.

Prohibitionists will predictably disagree, but so what? What right have alcohol drinkers, tobacco smokers, or non-drug users to decide on the importance of drug use to others? They have nothing but their own prejudice to support their opinions. Reason has never been brought to the table and so why should their bigotry, chauvinism and distorted worldview merit any consideration? What if we could find a billion people to whom outward appearance such as hair length was of little importance? Would their view in any way be representative for others? The courts have ruled time and again that this is an issue for the individual to decide, so why should drugs be otherwise? Why should alcohol drinkers, tobacco smokers and non-drug users be allowed to throw cannabis or opiate users in jail without ever providing good reasons? Why should the preconceived and deluded notions

---

selling drugs." Barnett, *Bad Trip* (1994) 4. This figure is supported by research gathered by Ostrowski in *The Moral and Practical Case for Drug Legalization* (1990) (648-50), where he concludes that some 40 percent of US murders are drug-law related. Professor Duke elaborates on similar findings: "In many cities, such as New Haven, Connecticut, at least half of the killings are drug-business related. Nationwide, between 5,000 and 10,000 murders per year are systemic to the drug business. Thus, more people are killed by the prohibition of drugs than by the drugs themselves." Duke, *Drug Prohibition: An Unnatural Disaster* (1995) 577 (sources omitted)

[159] Drug analyst James Ostrowski estimates that roughly 80% of the world's 200.000 drug-use-deaths are caused by prohibition while only 20% by the inherent qualities of the drugs. Ostrowski, *The Moral and Practical Case for Drug Legalization* (1990) 654. See also MIKALSEN, *TO END A WAR* (2015) n. 79-80 at 168-73

of fearful minds—of brains muddled by 100 years' worth of prohibitionist propaganda—be allowed to carry the day? What sort of justice system would allow such a travesty to continue decade after decade?

Unfortunately, the honest answer is that *only a society* in which the principle of equal protection carries the same weight as the off-track society portrayed in Orwell's *Animal Farm* would allow such a state of affairs. And the courts, therefore, could just as well, like the pigs in Orwell's classic novel, solemnly have declared that "Of course we are all equal, but some—like alcohol drinkers, tobacco smokers and non-drug users—are more equal than others."

While such analogies are never popularly embraced, the facts speak volumes. The cruel irony of the equality doctrine is that it discriminates against people based on irrelevant traits; that its application makes a mockery of law; and that all this is plain to see. "Plain to see," at least for justices capable of principled reasoning,[160] and yet, because "some are more alike," this charade can continue.

The inherent absurdity is made evident when we consider that in other situations, when the legislature enacts a law that burdens a segment of the population on basis of race or ethnic background, individuals associated with the group are

---

[160] As Justice Kobayashi of the Supreme Court of Hawaii noted: "The evidence indicates that the harms produced by the abusive use of marijuana are essentially of the same nature and quality as those produced by the abusive use of alcohol. As such, the failure to include alcohol within the criminally proscribed statutory classification could itself be considered violative of equal protection." *State v. Kantner*, 493 P.2d 306 (1972) at 320 (Kobayashi, J., dissenting). See also *State v. Mitchell*, 563 S.W.2d 18 (Mo. 1978) 37 (Shangler J., dissenting) ("I am convinced on impressive empirical authority that marihuana poses no threat to the public safety and welfare and less a danger to the person than that posed to the user of cigarettes and alcohol. There can be no reasonable basis to classify marihuana with narcotics or to penalize them alike. I would find that [the] classification of marihuana violates the equal protection clause of the Fourteenth Amendment to the United States Constitution and is invalid.")

entitled to a judicial determination that the burden they are asked to bear is precisely tailored to serve a compelling governmental interest. This is the case no matter how negligible the burden they are being asked to bear. Even if no criminal law is applied and the purpose of the legislation is to help a disadvantaged group, the Court will demand that the regulation be justified according to the most exacting criteria of scrutiny.[161] Why, then, are not drug users who risk lifetime imprisonment afforded the same courtesy? Why should the drug law—a law which arguably has had no less disastrous consequences than any race or ethnicity-based law—be exempt from the same level of review? Should not the millions of Americans who are imprisoned because of this law have a right to expect that it be precisely tailored to serve a compelling governmental interest? Or—if this is too much to ask—that, at the very least, it be *somewhat* tailored to achieve a legitimate purpose? What sort of justice system would deny even this? Why should drug users be left with no meaningful quality control? How is this fair?

A reply from prohibitionists is that the "suspect" classified groups are being asked to shoulder a burden based on a trait they can do nothing about, while drug users have chosen to exhibit behavior they know is prohibited. To some extent there is a difference between being criminalized for being black or Hispanic and for being a drug user. However, as seen, that people can avoid punishment by conforming to the demands of a law does not "eliminate concerns" about the importance of ensuring that the law is justified in the first place.

---

[161] *Adarand Constructors, Inc. v. Pena*, 515 U.S. 200 (1995), involving a federal affirmative action plan providing a benefit to minority contractors.

A second reply is that we have a hideous history with legislation that burdens a group based on traits of race or ethnicity, and that, to guard against the mistakes of the past, a law that separates people based on these criteria must pass strict scrutiny. This answer will provide us with proper justification for applying strict scrutiny to race-based legislation. However, it does not explain why drug users should not also be protected against discriminatory practices. After all, as a group they fulfill most criteria for being included in a suspect classification analysis. It is clear that the law directed against them were motivated by racism, ignorance, and prejudice; that it is a fear-based response to a perceived threat against the status quo; and that it burdens a politically inferior group.

Just like previous laws affecting race, the drug law is not only used to control a minority population but it serves to confirm and justify the prejudices and hypocrisies of the ingroup, making it appear legitimate to hate and despise the targeted population. Today, therefore, this class of people is so ostracized that it is politically acceptable to blame them for most evils. The very language that is used in political debates, courts, and media outlets to describe "the problem" leaves no doubt. In our modern-day caste system, they are the "untouchables," the "vermin," the "pushers," and the ones infested by the "plague." They are those designated to the lowest rung on the social ladder and delegated the unbearable task of atoning for the sins of others.

We shall have more to say on this aspect of prohibition, but the sentencing practices clearly reveal that when it comes to these "misfits" anything goes. The horrendous effect that the drug law has had on the lives of tens of millions of people is simply too unfathomable to grasp. But we can begin by acknowledging that these millions are real people; they have names. They are people like Robert Zornes and his wife, Jenice, both 22 years, who were lying on the lawn watching meteors on the night sky when about half a dozen officers raided their home. After uncovering a tiny amount of marijuana on the premises, the government sentenced Robert to 20 years while Jenice "got off" with one year. They are people like David Ciglar, a firefighter credited with saving over 100 lives and also a husband and father of three. Ciglar got a mandatory minimum of 10 years after being caught with a tray of marijuana seedlings in his garage and his family home was confiscated. They are people like James Geddes, who was sentenced to 90 years after police found a small amount of marijuana and five plants in his vegetable garden. They are people like James Cox, who discovered the therapeutic effects of marijuana after struggling with cancer. He was sentenced to 15 years for growing his own medicine; his wife, Pat, got 5 years and they also lost the family house. They are people like Will Foster, a husband and father of three who struggled with crippling rheumatoid arthritis. He was sentenced to 93 years in prison for his attempt to find relief through cannabis—a sentence that was later reduced to 20 years. They are people like Jodie Israel and Calvin Treiber, a couple who belonged to a religious community that used marijuana as a sacrament. Jodie was sentenced to 11 years while Calvin received a 29-year sentence for possessing smaller amounts of the herb. Their four children were orphaned by the government and separated from each other to live in different homes.[162]

---

[162] For more on these and many more examples of the victims of the War on Drugs, see CONRAD, NORRIS & RESNER, *HUMAN RIGHTS AND THE US DRUG WAR* (2001)

While the courts' equal protection doctrine allows for this, the Equal Protection Clause does not. The equality guarantee inherent in the Constitution seeks to remove from existence all laws that serve the interests of a particular class rather than the general public (class legislation) and to eliminate all statutes that subject one class of citizens to a code not applicable to another. The Clause is connected to the fundamental principles of justice and these principles care not one bit if rights are termed "fundamental" or classifications are called "suspect." They simply demand that *all* infringements on liberty be reasonable, and they demand that all groups singled out for persecution shall have their day in court.

Recognizing this, there is no reason why laws directed at drug users should be held to a lesser standard than laws directed at blacks, women, or homosexuals.[163] The right not to be unduly deprived of autonomy and liberty is fundamental. And while the examples above may belong to the extreme end, they are certainly not unique. In fact, we can multiply the pain and suffering of these people and their families by a million before we come close to putting the cruelty of the drug law in its proper perspective. Why, then, is the suffering of these people reduced to insignificance? Where in all this is the right to equal respect and concern? The equal protection test is simple: Would we accept alcohol drinkers or tobacco smokers being treated like this?

---

[163] Justice Marshall has argued that "the level of scrutiny employed in an equal protection case should vary with 'the constitutional and societal importance of the interest adversely affected and the recognized invidiousness of the basis upon which the particular classification is drawn." *City of Cleburne v. Cleburne Living Ctr.*, 473 U.S. 432, 460 (Marshall, J., dissenting in part) (quoting San Antonio Independent School District v. Rodriguez, 411 U. S. 1, 411 U. S. 99 (1973)

There is evidence to suggest that we would not. Not only does reason forbid it, but the European Court of Human Rights looked into the issue of depriving alcohol users their liberty rights in *Witold Litwa v. Polen*. The Court concluded that even a couple hours in a holding cell was unconstitutional and so we have an idea of the different measures of decency applied towards the two groups of people. But why is it so difficult to understand that the drug law violators have an equal right to liberty? Why is it impossible to accept to this group the same measure of human dignity?

To find the answer, we must look to the enemy image of drugs.

2.5. The Impact of an Overblown Enemy Image

Studies reveal that the more we know about illicit drugs, the less scary they become.[164] In fact, in comparing the harms associated with tobacco and alcohol to those of illicit drugs, we find that we have legalized the drugs that are the worst for society (alcohol) and the most addictive and harmful to the individual (tobacco).[165]

According to Duke and Gross, per 100,000 users, tobacco kills 650 people each year, alcohol 150, heroin 80, cocaine 4, and marijuana zero.[166] The most comprehensive study done on the harms associated with the different drugs confirms this picture. In this study the Independent Scientific Committee on Drugs compared each drug to 16 criteria of harm. On a

---

[164] BAKALAR & GRINSPOON, *DRUG CONTROL IN A FREE SOCIETY* (1998) 17

[165] MIKALSEN, *TO END A WAR* (2015) notes 70-72 at 154-62

[166] DUKE & GROSS, *AMERICA'S LONGEST WAR* (1993) 74-77

scale from zero to 100, where zero was the most favourable outcome and 100 was the worst possible, they came up with a ranking that looked like this: Psychedelic mushrooms (6), Buprenorphine (7), LSD (7), Khat (9), Ecstasy (9), Anabolic Steroids (10), Butane (11), Mephedrone (13), Methadone (14), Ketamine (15), Benzodiazepines (15), GHB (19), Cannabis (20), Amphetamine (23), Tobacco (26), Cocaine (27), Methylamphetamine (33), Crack (54), Heroin (55), and Alcohol (72).[167]

As we can see, there is no relation between the overall harmfulness of these drugs and their classification. In fact, in most cases the classification is completely backwards, as some of the least dangerous drugs are the most strictly prohibited.

Predictably, many people will disagree with the conclusions reached by the ISCD. After all, we live in a world where the prohibition ideology has shaped our minds to such an extent that most of us simply cannot accept these findings. That alcohol could be more dangerous than heroin and tobacco more dangerous than LSD is so contradictory to common beliefs that most automatically discard such findings. Nonetheless, the more we learn about drugs, the more likely we are to agree.[168]

The more we know, the more we understand that the same supply and demand mechanisms are involved when it comes to the licit and illicit drugs; that there are the same

---

[167] Nutt et al., *Drug harms in the UK: a Multicriteria Decision Analysis*, LANCET 2010: 376, at 1558–65

[168] As Professor Escohotado noted: "[In the ten-year period after its prohibition] up to twenty million may have been introduced to LSD in the United States and Europe, and the number of crimes or fatal accidents caused by its use in that decade hardly reached that produced by alcohol in one single day." ESCOHOTADO, *A BRIEF HISTORY OF DRUGS* (1999) 123

varying patterns of use; and that the illicit drugs are no worse than the licit. In fact, some of them hold enormous potential for psychological healing/growth and can be of immense value to society.[169] And the more we come to terms with this factual picture, the more we also come to grips with its implications—that the classification system that separates licit and illicit drugs makes no sense, and that the basis of the War on Drugs is fundamentally flawed.[170]

Prohibitionists, however, are not there. The enemy image of drugs is deeply ingrained, and, as knowledge brings us closer to the FC level while ignorance and fear drags us down to the NC level, it comes as no surprise where prohibitionist reasoning is found. Due to the exaggerated enemy image, they will apply two diametrically opposed types of reasoning to the two classes of drugs—and while they recognize alcohol and tobacco consumers as autonomous individuals responsible for their lifestyle choices, they see illicit drug consumers as the victims of sinister influences, meaning cynical dope peddlers and the lure of an easy fix.

This is the myth that sustains the ideology of prohibition. Without this foundation, it would be impossible to infantilize adults and persecute them for using their drugs of choice.

---

[169] Not only are the psychedelic drugs unique tools in the rehabilitation of drug addicts but in helping us overcome dysfunctional, deeply flawed, but commonly accepted outlooks on life. They can, in short, help us become full FC individuals. See MIKALSEN, *REASON IS* (2014); FORTE, *ENTHEOGENS AND THE FUTURE OF RELIGION* (2012); GRAY, *THE ACID DIARIES* (2010); SMITH, *CLEANSING THE DOORS OF PERCEPTION* (2000); GROF, *REALMS OF THE HUMAN UNCONSCIOUS* (1975); GROF, *LSD: DOORWAY TO THE NUMINOUS* (2009); GOLDSMITH, *PSYCHEDELIC HEALING* (2010); WINKELMAN & ROBERTS (EDS.), *PSYCHEDELIC MEDICINE* (2007); GRINSPOON & BAKALAR, *PSYCHEDELIC DRUGS RECONSIDERED* (1997); GROF, *THE COSMIC GAME: EXPLORATIONS OF THE FRONTIERS OF HUMAN CONSCIOUSNESS* (1990); STRASSMAN, *DMT: THE SPIRIT MOLECULE* (2001); Tupper & Labate, *Plants, Psychoactive Substances and the International Narcotics Control Board* (2012); Watts, *Psychedelics and Religious Experience* (1968); *supra* note 95

[170] MIKALSEN, *TO END A WAR* (2015) n. 70-75 at 154-65

Without it, the demonization of those involved with the drugs economy would be understood as the mindless endeavor it is. And without it, the cruelty of our sentencing practices would be plain to see.

We shall now see how the courts are colored by this fiction.

2.5.1. Prohibitionist Reasoning Writ Large

Prohibitionist reasoning in its pure form was most prevalent in the first half of the 20th century. The narcotics police were the purveyors of information and as neither the legislature nor the courts knew anything about these drugs, they fell prey to the Federal Bureau of Narcotics' misinformation campaigns. According to the *Burke* court, it was "an established fact" that "narcotic drugs are dangerous. Not that they are poisons within themselves, but worse than poisons. Their excessive use destroys will power, ambition, self-respect, and in the end, mentality. They make men and women moral perverts."[171]

"Narcotic drugs" included cannabis, and we saw another example of the influence of this enemy image in *Markham*. In this case the defendant sought an opportunity to dispel the myths surrounding marijuana, proving it was no "narcotic" and therefore should not be classified among the hard drugs. Circuit Judge Duffy, however, held that it was a narcotic because Congress had decided it was a narcotic and that it belonged to the class of hard drugs because the legislature had decided it belonged there. As proof of the harmful effects of

---

[171] *Burke v. Kansas State Osteopathic Assoc., Inc.*, 111 F.2d 250, 256 (1940)

marijuana, he cited the following text from the legislature's deliberations:

> "Marihuana is . . . used illicitly by smoking it in crudely prepared cigarettes, which are readily procurable in almost all parts of the country at prices ranging from 10 to 25 cents each. Under the influence of this drug the will is destroyed and all power of directing and controlling thought is lost. As a result of these effects many violent crimes have been and are being committed by persons under the influence of the drug. Not only is marihuana used by hardened criminals to steel them to commit violent crimes, but it is also being placed in the hands of high school children in the form of marihuana cigarettes by unscrupulous peddlers. Its continued use results many times in impotency and insanity."[172]

The enemy image of drugs having such an influence, it comes as no surprise that several states made the death penalty available for those who delivered drugs to adolescents. It also comes as no surprise that in *Thomas*, the first challenge raising the issue of cruel and unusual punishment, the Louisiana Supreme Court upheld that state's mandatory minimum sentence of ten years without parole for unlawful possession. As the court said, "[i]n view of the moral degeneration inherent in all aspects of the crime denounced by the Narcotics Act, it cannot be said that the length or severity of the punishment here prescribed is disproportioned to the offense."[173] Five years later, in *Garcia*,

---

[172] *United States v. Markham*, C07.126, 191 F.2d 936 (1951)

[173] *State v. Thomas*, 224 La. 435, 69 So.2d 740 (1953). Seven years later, in *Gallego v. United States*, the Ninth Circuit quoted approvingly this moral denouncement when it decided in favor of a five-year minimum for the possession of drugs.

the Texas Supreme Court upheld a life sentence for first offense possession.[174] But even if the moral climate supported the severity of such punishment (and has continued to do so until this day), there were a distinct change in the air. As drug use became more widespread throughout the 1960s, an increasing amount of research and information became available. By 1970, between ten and fifteen percent of the American people had tried marijuana and it was plain to see that prohibitionists had misrepresented the factual picture.

The courts would increasingly draw upon this knowledge to reject the government's version of events. In 1970, in *State v. Zornes*, the Supreme Court of Washington was the first to find marijuana laws unconstitutional on classification grounds.[175] In 1971, in *People v. McCabe*, the Supreme Court of Illinois followed and concluded that the classification of marijuana with the hard drugs violated the equal protection clause of the Fourteenth Amendment. One year later, in *People v. Sinclair*, the Supreme Court of Michigan dealt another blow to the drug law. Delivering the opinion of the court, Justice Swainson affirmed that:

> "Comparison of the effects of marijuana use on both the individual and society with the effects of other drug use demonstrates not only that there is no rational basis for classifying marijuana with the 'hard narcotics', but, also, that there is not even a rational basis for treating marijuana as a more dangerous drug than alcohol. . . . The murky atmosphere of ignorance and misinformation

---

[174] *Garcia v. State*, 166 Tex. Crim. 482, 316 S.-AV.2d 734 (1958)

[175] The court held that the law was arbitrary and irrational. Before this trial courts in Colorado had twice declared the state's marijuana laws unconstitutional but had been reversed both times. *People v. McKenzie*, 458 P.2d 232 (Colo. 1969); *People v. Stark*, 157 Colo. 59.400 P.2d 923 (1965)

which casts its pall over the state and Federal legislatures' original classification of marijuana with the hard narcotics has been well documented . . . We can no longer allow the residuals of that early misinformation to continue choking off a rational evaluation of marijuana dangers. That a large and increasing number of Americans recognize the truth about marijuana's relative harmlessness can scarcely be doubted. . . . We agree with the Illinois Supreme Court . . . that marijuana is improperly classified as a narcotic and hold that [the law], in its classification of marijuana violates the equal protection clauses of the [state and Federal Constitution]."[176]

As the 1970s unfolded, more and more courts would recognize the relative harmlessness of cannabis. The pressure for reform was growing and many scholars expected prohibition to yield.[177] However, they underestimated the prohibitionists' will to power and ignorance, and despite the incriminating evidence the enemy image held sway.

The *Sinclair* court, for instance, did not properly digest the implications of the passage above, as the court refused to look into the more important issues. Sinclair, a political

---

[176] *People v. Sinclair*, 387 Mich. 91, 194 N.W.2d 878 (1972) at 104-115

[177] "A fundamental alteration of drug policy, particularly with regard to marijuana, is inevitable. . . . Yet despite an overwhelming volume of scientific criticism of existing law, legislatures have taken only token action. The source of the law is now its defense—ignorance. Even though independent researchers have disproved all of the old assumptions, the status quo is maintained on the ground that the evidence is not yet in on long-range effects of repeated use. A poor basis for a criminal law in any case, this argument is defectively open-ended. . . . If the legislative process continues to stall . . . we predict that the judiciary will no longer restrain itself. . . . Although we would prefer that the courts not be forced to enter still another political thicket, we do believe . . . that a declaration of unconstitutionality is analytically justifiable." Bonnie & Whitebread, *The Forbidden Fruit and the Tree of Knowledge* (1970) 1170

activist of regional notoriety, had originally contended that the statute (among other things) violated equal protection, denied due process of law, violated rights of privacy retained by the people, and that the penalty provisions imposed cruel and unusual punishment. In all, he raised ten constitutional objections, but the court dealt only with two. One being whether the classification of marijuana as a narcotic violated the equal protection guarantee of the Constitution and the other being whether the two marijuana cigarettes Sinclair was charged with should have been excluded from evidence on the ground that they constituted evidence obtained as the result of an illegal police entrapment. The court concluded in the affirmative on both accounts and reversed Sinclair's ten-year sentence.

Only one of the justices, T.G. Kavanagh, had the acumen to point out that the court had neglected the obvious—the defective relationship to first principles. As he held:

"Although I am persuaded that our statute is unconstitutional, I cannot agree that my Brothers have ascribed the correct or even permissible reasons for this conclusion. . . . I find that our statute violates the Federal and State Constitutions in that it is an impermissible intrusion on the fundamental rights to liberty and the pursuit of happiness, and is an unwarranted interference with the right to possess and use private property. As I understand our constitutional concept of government, an individual is free to do whatever he pleases, so long as he does not interfere with the rights of his neighbor or of society, and no government state or Federal has been ceded the authority to interfere with that freedom."[178]

Again, we see principled reasoning in effect, and from this period we have other examples of this more highly evolved perspective. These justices, however, belonged to a minority and the majority would be too enmeshed in the enemy image of drugs to connect with first principles. Hence, despite the efforts of dissenters, constitutional challenges would fail time and again.

Even so, things would go from bad to worse, for as the 1970s ended the enemy image of drugs was reinflated to its former glory. The Reagan and Bush Administrations militarized the War on Drugs and would use this enemy image for all its worth. To succeed, a revision of history was necessary and 64 different catalogues and information pamphlets from the National Institute of Drug Abuse were removed from public libraries.[179] Drug taking was no longer accepted as a health problem. It was purely a moral problem, one that was explained by a lack of character, social commitment, and decency. Also, there was no longer a difference between soft and hard drugs; they were all the same and *all drug use* equaled abuse.

The government's misinformation machine worked in high gear and a predictable moral panic ensued. As psychologists have discovered, only those individuals found at the more advanced stages of psychological growth have some measure of immunity against propaganda efforts, and even though drug use rates had dropped for five years in a row, polls from 1989 revealed that 62 percent of the American

---

[178] *People v. Sinclair*, 387 Mich. 91, 194 N.W.2d 878 (1972) at 132-33

[179] BAUM, *SMOKE AND MIRRORS* (1996) 164

people were willing to give up more of their freedoms in the war against drugs. 83 percent also responded that reporting drug taking friends and family members to the police was the proper thing to do,[180] for as America's drug czar, William Bennett, had told them: "Turning in one's friends, is an act of true loyalty—of true friendship."[181] Bennett, a professor who used to teach ethics, also confirmed that he had "no moral qualms about beheading convicted drug dealers."[182]

It is not for nothing that Professor Wisotsky has described prohibition as "profoundly totalitarian."[183] Even ministers of the Church would join the choir calling for the death penalty,[184] and the enemy image of drugs being reestablished there was, as we can expect, a marked drop in principled reasoning. As demonstrated in *To Right a Wrong*, there is a connection between the two in the sense that they are polar opposites. On the one hand, the more enlightened we become, the less impact an enemy image will have, and on the other, the more powerful an enemy image becomes, the further we will draw towards those stages that illustrate the lower levels of cognitive evolution.

Psychologically speaking, it is difficult to overestimate the power of enemy images. They appeal to our emotions, not our intellect; they affect us in primordial ways, and their impact is such that people will prefer ignorance to knowledge.

---

[180] Ibid. 245, 277

[181] Ibid. 280

[182] L.A. Times, *Beheading of Convicted Drug Dealers Discussed by Bennett*, June 16, 1989

[183] DUKE & CROSS, *AMERICA'S LONGEST WAR* (1993) 159

[184] As Reverend Jesse Jackson stated: "Since the flow of drugs into the U.S. is an act of terrorism, antiterrorist policies must be applied. . . . If someone is transmitting the death agent to Americans, that person should face wartime consequences. The line must be drawn." SZASZ, *OUR RIGHT TO DRUGS* (1992) 113

A principled review of reality tends to be avoided at all costs, because the enemy image does not only provide an outlet for subconscious fears—it also provides an identity.

2.5.2. The Psychological Dimension

"The fact that drug use can be discussed at the highest levels of government only in metaphorical terms with mythological demonic imagery constitutes an unmistakable warning to us that something is seriously wrong."[185]

—Judge Sweet & Edward Harris—

The language and the confused reasoning that accompanies the prohibition ideology, coupled with the fervency with which the persecution of drug users is administered, betrays that something else is afoot. It suggests that psychological defense mechanisms are at play which are rarely understood and to overcome the power of enemy images, these psychological issues must be clarified.

We have already seen that for those in the grips of an enemy image the suggestion of reevaluating the presumptions from which they build a worldview is met with great resistance. The reasons will soon be explained, but it is impossible to understand the history of constitutional challenges without adding the psychological dimension. Only this can explain why drug prohibition has endured to this day unsupported by evidence and reason. Only this can explain

---

[185] Sweet & Harris, *Moral and Constitutional Considerations in Support of the Decriminalization of Drugs*, in FISH (ED.), *HOW TO LEGALIZE DRUGS* (1998) 432

the doublethink[186] and cognitive dissonance that allows for different kinds of logic to be applied to otherwise similar cases. And only this can explain why judges and lawyers who normally take great pride in the respectability of their profession will undermine the rule of law rather than let drug users have their day in court.

Now, due to the impact of the enemy image (and the psychological incentives behind it), most individuals will not perceive it this way. Nonetheless, if the previous pages have not yet convinced the reader, further documentation will be provided—and to those sufficiently free from the bias and prejudices that cloud so many contemporary minds, all this is embarrassingly clear. As Professor Wisotsky summarized the judiciary's treatment of drug cases:

> "What is remarkable is the extent to which the irratio-nality [of the legislature] is shared by the judicial branch, the branch institutionally committed to knowledge and reason. . . . Judges who have been called upon to answer drug law policy questions . . . have abandoned the method of fact-based, reasoned elaboration that is the essence of

---

[186] "Doublethink" is the act of simultaneously accepting two mutually contradictory beliefs as correct. It is related to cognitive dissonance but somewhat more serious, for while the latter reflects a condition where contradictory beliefs cause a certain conflict in one's mind, the doublethinker is unaware of any conflict or contradiction. In other words, (to paraphrase Wiki-pedia) doublethinking is the act of relieving cognitive dissonance by ignoring the contradiction between two incompatible world views—or even of deliberately seeking to relieve cognitive dissonance. As Orwell observed: "To know and not to know, to be conscious of complete truthfulness while telling carefully constructed lies, to hold simultaneously two opinions which cancelled out, knowing them to be contradictory and believing in both of them, to use logic against logic, to repudiate morality while laying claim to it, . . . to forget whatever it was necessary to forget, then to draw it back into memory again at the moment when it was needed, and then promptly to forget it again, and above all, to apply the same process to the process itself—that was the ultimate subtlety: consciously to induce unconsciousness, and then, once again, to become unconscious of the act of hypnosis you had just performed." ORWELL, NINETEEN EIGHTY-FOUR (1949) 32

thinking like a lawyer or deciding like a judge. In place of careful analysis, judges have attempted to justify drug law decisions with misinformation or inflammatory rhetoric. ... Few opinions combine careful reasoning and attention to evidence or empirical knowledge; we are left instead with drug law decisions based mainly on metaphors of outrage at drug users and sellers. Courts denounce the 'degeneracy' of 'moral perverts,' and call them 'vampires' or the 'walking dead' engaged in 'ugly' and 'insidious' drug distribution offenses. Generations of scientific research, scholarly analysis, and the reports of learned commissions have been almost completely ignored. The Supreme Court of the United States has never cited . . . any of the classic drug policy studies . . . in opinions concerning drug laws. Instead, [its opinions are] filled with emotionally charged dicta mimicking the political rhetoric that has dominated drug control in the United States since its inception. ... In this respect, they have damaged the ethical basis of the adversary system, converting it largely into a propaganda tool for the party line."[187]

That the Supreme Court has abandoned all pretense of objectivity in this area is not even denied. As Justice Stevens himself said, "No impartial observer could criticize this Court for hindering the progress of the War on Drugs."[188] He even took pride in calling the Court a "loyal foot soldier in the Executive's fight,"[189] and to explain why otherwise upright judges so consistently embrace populist bias and let prejudice

---

[187] Wisotsky, *Not thinking Like a Lawyer* (1991)

[188] *California v. Acevedo*, U.S. slip op. 17 (1991) (Stevens J., dissenting)

[189] Id.

take the place of reason, some important psychological factors bear emphasis.

One is what Mill called the tyranny of majority opinion. After more than 100 years of prohibition, its ideology has transcended the factual realm. The premises upon which it rests have been elevated to the status of myth, and the power of myth is simply too immense for most to resist.[190]

Today, therefore, everyone knows that "drugs are bad" and the fact that drug prohibition came into being as a result of irrational fears, racism, and insufficient knowledge is conveniently forgotten. I say "conveniently," for as the prohibition philosophy has shaped society, the powers that be have developed such vested interest in this ideology (and maintaining the overblown enemy image behind it) that no amount of evidence as to the destructive effects of their crusade has succeeded in changing their minds.

This, however, is only one side of the coin and on the other we must recognize that drug users fulfill an important social role. Throughout history people have had a need to find some outsider-group (1) to use as a measure of their own wholesomeness, and (2) to blame for the ills that befall society. If we look closer, this has been the emotional appeal behind every mass-movement gone wrong and drug prohibition is no different; it persists because it separates the

---

[190] If the power of myth is not already apparent in the irrational fears and the incomprehensible logic that drives the War on Drugs, then it should be plain to recognize in its end, the dream of a drug free society. Even though the drug war has only succeeded in bringing us further away from this imagined ideal, it is still being held up by prohibitionists as the end of their righteous quest, and just like a mirage in the desert can make deluded men run towards their death so the pursuit of this ever-elusive ideal has brought society ever closer to its demise. In pursuit of this ideal, we have thrown the Constitution out the window as the "drug exception" to the Bill of Rights keeps broadening the police power. If not for the power of myth alarm bells would ring out by this unfolding process, but instead it has been accepted as a necessary evil.

world into us versus them, providing an outlet for unconscious fears.

The psychological incentive behind our eagerness to separate the world into us and them results from the fact that a person cannot live without having some measure of self-worth. Neither organized religion nor Neo-Darwinism can provide us with a sound footing and so people will have to look elsewhere to solve this problem. Unless they embrace the mystics' perspective on religion/spirituality, there is one way to do this, and it is finding someone to look down on. Hence, if people are not sufficiently free from the collective Groupmind to go with the mystics' option, this is what they will do. It may be homosexuals, drug users, a racial group, whatever; the important thing is that *something out there must serve as a measure of lesser-worth* so that people can experience themselves as having at least some relative value. The more they are troubled by feelings of inadequate self-worth, the greater will be the psychological incentive to trample others down, and as soon as a group has been targeted for this purpose the process of degradation begins. The moral status of those in the outgroup will be bitterly attacked and their humanity eroded until the moral obligations we sense towards our fellow men no longer apply. All those qualities we refuse to accept within ourselves, all our repressed fears, will be projected onto this outsider group—and to the extent that we can see them at the "other," this something that we are not, we will bring meaning to the image of our own goodness.

This outsider group will be blamed for the problems of society and it becomes self-evident that they must be removed. No matter the time and place, this is the recipe behind any mass-movement gone wrong—and in this sense drug users are the modern equivalent of witches, Jews, and other social outcasts. This is well-known among scholars,[191] and according to this view, owing to our fear of having to accept responsibility for ourselves and our actions as free and rational agents, we have located the source of our problems in drugs.

We have seen that in the State there will be a constant pressure from above to deprive us of autonomy. Agents of the state will encourage dependency and paternalistic policies, and while this can be a comfortable solution, it is a Faustian bargain that will come back to haunt us. Not only is it a law of politics that tyrannical government will ensue if we fail to take responsibility for our lives, but dereliction of our duty as adults to take responsibility for our own behaviors and lifestyle choices will undermine our feelings of self-worth. This is inevitable, for to the extent we conform to the State's expectations, we must abandon that which makes us individuals—our penchant for autonomy, freedom, and responsibility. To the extent we reject these values we will be less than complete individuals. We will be living on our knees, submitting to the rule of others, and we will be secretly ashamed of ourselves.

I say "secretly," as none of this can be admitted. We will continue to see ourselves as sovereign agents and in no way

---

[191] Professors of law, philosophy, and psychiatry have demonstrated that the drug war in its essence is a religious crusade and that the modern persecution of drugs, drug users, and pushers must be seen against the historical backdrop of the ritual persecution of other scapegoats such as heretics, witches, Jews, and madmen. SEE SZASZ, *CEREMONIAL CHEMISTRY* (2003). See also HUSAK, *DRUGS AND RIGHTS* (1992); MILLER, *THE CASE FOR LEGALIZING DRUGS* (1991) 109-24; Stuart, *War as Metaphor and the Rule of Law in Crisis* (2011); Levine & Reinarman, *The Transition from Prohibition to Regulation: Lessons from Alcohol Policy for Drug Policy*, in FISH (ED.), *HOW TO LEGALIZE DRUGS* (1998); Somerville: *Stigmatization, scapegoating and discrimination in sexually transmitted diseases: overcoming "them" and "us"* (1994)

acknowledge the extent to which we fall short of this ideal. This phenomenon is well-known,[192] and it should come as no surprise that people who reject autonomy in their own life feel deeply threatened by those who take its value more seriously.

Thus, drug users become so deeply despised. For one, drug use is associated with youth culture. Adolescents have an ingrained opposition to false authority, a yearning for freedom, and the courage to act on it. Fretting about all this has always been a favorite pastime of the elder generation for in the youth they are confronted with the reality of their own souls. This is a most difficult encounter. While the elder generation at some point shared the youth's impatience with false authority, their social conditioning and careers have made them cognitively weak and morally corrupt. The price they have paid for conformity is accepting a social contract based on lies, oppression, and injustice, and this is not easily admitted. Therefore, most adults go through life with eyes wide shut, willfully neglecting the obvious. Reality must be avoided at all costs and they will stick with the established paradigm—the idea that (1) the current state of affairs is not that bad; (2) that to the extent there are problems to be solved their authorities are working on it; (3) that improvement takes time (in the sense, who knows when?); (4) that the only responsible way of action is to work within the system to improve things; (5) that rejecting the authority of those in

---

[192] To paraphrase Miller: "To live what Joseph Campbell calls an 'authentic life' people must consciously choose one of the alternatives—irresponsibility or autonomy. Many people refuse to make a conscious choice. They refuse to admit that their lives repudiate autonomy. Rather than face reality, they choose to live a lie. The result is mental illness, as guilt grows about betrayal of moral ideas. This personal guilt cannot be faced (otherwise people could make a conscious choice). Yet an outlet must be found. Drug addicts become natural scapegoats for wrath; they do freely what their fellow citizens do in shame. Drug addicts personify what Americans hate about themselves." MILLER, *THE CASE FOR LEGALIZING DRUGS* (1991) 111

charge is not a sensible option; and (6) that those who do are irresponsible and immature troublemakers.

This is the mindset that goes with being a well-adjusted citizen. And as these citizens do not have the courage to oppose false authority, they fret about the younger generation. This psychological response is only natural, as they themselves at some level are aware that something is rotten in the kingdom. Thus, they are deeply uncomfortable when faced with any reminder of the treason they have committed in accepting a social contract on false pretenses. To protect from this embarrassment, they instinctively reject questions or behaviors that rock the boat—and as the youth cannot be blamed for cherishing wholesome values, they are abused for their drug preferences. Because they have qualms about authority, and still own the integrity to demand some meaningful measure of control over their lives, that percentage of the population who blindly accept the power of authority will side with authority in these perceived acts of rebellion. It is well-known that drug use to many people is an expression of liberation rather than enslavement. By using these drugs responsibly and to their satisfaction they not only dispel the propaganda that authority rely on to keep the populace sedated; they refute the fundamental premise of the crusade—the hilarious notion that authority persecutes them for their own good.[193]

No wonder this act of insolence is deeply frowned upon. Their activities are a reminder that those who side with

---

[193] As Miller noted, "drug users . . . demonstrate the sincerity of their belief in personal freedom by persisting in free choice of drugs even at the risk of arrest and imprisonment. That kind of moral courage contrasts with elders who fear even the right to choose. Youths challenge the validity of orders that other citizens want to obey. Youths who act as they live in a democracy generate hatred among citizens who fear democracy." MILLER, *THE CASE FOR LEGALIZING DRUGS* (1991) 117

authority build their lives on a lie, and so they are persecuted for representing those values preached but abandoned by the elder generation. Because this generation cannot face the fact that rebellion, suicide, crime, depression, and misbehavior among the youth are no more than symptoms of the extent to which society fails to live up to social contract thinking, they must find some other cause to explain all this—and so drugs, music, and the like, will be blamed.[194]

Thus, scapegoating drug users is intimately connected with these "well-adjusted" citizens' inability to face the Faustian bargain that comes with being compliant members of a deeply unjust society. The problem of "dangerous drugs" becomes the answer, an escape clause, that makes the otherwise unfaceable possible to ignore. Even if drug prohibition has failed in its explicitly stated purpose it has succeeded exceptionally well in this regard. The myth of the "demon drugs" has made it possible for the average citizen to keep a cognitive discord intact by ignoring reality and making the victims bear the oppressor's guilt. No one else—not robbers, rapists, or murderers—is hated as are drug users, and the minimum penalties imposed by U.S. Federal law illustrate this level of fear, as well as the insanity that results: Burglary with a gun—2.0 years; kidnapping—4.2 years; rape—5.8

---

[194] Hence, as Bakalar and Grinspoon observed, the reason why we prohibit drug use is analogous to the reason why Iranians prohibit Western music. In Iran, listening to Western music is seen as an act of rebellion against the establishment and the way it handles social problems. In the same way, drug use in our society it is taken as a personal threat to those who support the status quo. The people in charge, whether it be of Western or Iranian society, will always see themselves as preservers of all that is decent and worthwhile. Change is regarded as a threat to their powerbase and so, to them, music and drug use represents an objectionable way of life, one that is characterized by unproductive behavior, unreliability, dishonesty, lack of moral values, and anti-authoritarian tendencies. BAKALAR & GRINSPOON, *DRUG CONTROL IN A FREE SOCIETY* (1998) 19

years; attempted murder—6.5 years; possession of LSD—
10.1 years![195]

It is no coincidence that the less we know, the easier it
becomes to believe in the demonizing traits that is ascribed to
the "other;" the greater impact the enemy image will have on
our minds; the more we will despise and fear the perceived
"enemy;" and the more efficiently this enemy image will
provide its psychological function, which is absolve us from
"sin." When it comes to this psychological set-up ignorance,
fear, and disgust feed off each other, and for the sake of
"sanity" reason cannot be allowed. If prohibitionists were to
reconsider the underlying premises of their assumptions, they
would no longer have straw men to attack. Instead, they
would have to face their fears and inadequacies head on—and
they would have to come to terms with the horrible truth of
their campaign, which is too disturbing to consider.

We must remember that the problem to begin with is an
ego unsure of itself and that psychological growth (which
always equals more love for self and others) is needed before
they can face reality. Consequently, they will strongly reject
any attempt to have reality imposed on them or their policies.
No matter the historical context this psychological set-up is
the same, and it is no easier for a prohibitionist to come to
terms with the reality of his campaign than it was for a Nazi
or an inquisitionist. This being so, unless we are to look for
more sinister motives, the hysteria and absurd reasoning that
goes with the prohibition ideology is a testimony to the power
of the unconscious, for when the truth becomes unbearable
defense mechanisms will intervene to keep us from putting
two and two together.

---

[195] SZASZ, *CEREMONIAL CHEMISTRY* (2003) 188

Now, most people are oblivious to such psychological influences. They know that they despise drug users (and hate drug distributors) but they do not know why, and they will look for rational reasons to explain irrational opinions. As we shall see, the enemy image dictates the logic and not the other way around, and so they will be looking for evidence that confirms their opinions: they will reason from worse-case scenarios; they will rely on hearsay and flawed research; and they will ignore all evidence to the contrary. So it is that even today, nearly fifty years after Professor Kaplan, after a two-year study of the drug law, concluded that the arguments relied upon by prohibitionists "are often so transparently flimsy that one can hardly believe they have been put forward seriously,"[196] continue to regurgitate the very same logic, even though the evidence to refute it has grown exponentially.

This is the power of enemy images and the psychological incentives behind them. It is simply taken for granted that one knows what one knows, and as long as they remain in the grip of these influences prohibitionists will degrade any constitutional challenge to the point where, as the Supreme Court held in *Chapman*, "whatever debate there is [will] center around the appropriate sentence and not the criminality of the conduct."[197] It is simply impossible for these judges to take seriously the notion that drug use could be a constitutionally protected activity as it would open the floodgates to self-reflection. Hence, as other commentators have noted, the sloppy reasoning that is applied in drug cases

---

[196] KAPLAN, *MARIJUANA: THE NEW PROHIBITION* (1971) 3

[197] *Chapman v. United States*, 500 U.S. 453 (1991)

is a testimony to the psychological bias that serves to deny users a fair trial,[198] and we shall now explore this bit.

2.5.3. The Problem of Differently Applied Logic

"An extraterrestrial creature who listened to our declarations about the terrible problems created by drugs, and then compared our approach to marijuana with alcohol and tobacco, would have to conclude that we do not quite mean what we are saying."[199]

—James Bakalar & Lester Grinspoon—

From what we have seen, it is evident that prohibition can only be taken seriously by those found at the lower levels of human growth. Indeed, from the higher perspective it is a symptom of the psychological traits that define a less-evolved mindset, as only a society populated by individuals scared of embracing the responsibility that comes with being an adult would accept the premises of drug prohibition. The reasoning that accompanies the prohibitionist mindset is characteristic of the lower-analytical faculties of those inhabiting the lower levels of the FC/NC model (as described in *To Right a Wrong*),[200] and for those inhabiting the higher-end it is

---

[198] Brashear, *Marijuana Prohibition and the Constitutional Right of Privacy* (1975) 575 ("the brevity of the treatment suggests that these courts not only considered the right of privacy in general to be somewhat suspect, but also assumed that the argument was not seriously offered by defendant.")

[199] BAKALAR & GRINSPOON, *DRUG CONTROL IN A FREE SOCIETY* (1998) 131

[200] The FC/NC Model tracks increasing consciousness-levels in the population. Building on data from psychology, it places societies and individuals at different levels of maturity/cognition, ranging from the isolated, fear-filled perspective found at the NC-end to the wholeness-oriented, loving perspective found at the FC-end.

perceived as the folly it is. For instance, the modern-day decision to deny drugs status as property is just ridiculous as seen from the higher perspective, for as James Madison said: "In its larger and juster meaning, [property] embraces everything to which a man may attach a value . . . [and includes that] which individuals have in their opinions, their religion, their passions, and their faculties."[201]

On this notion alone, the distinction between licit and illicit drugs is illegitimate. As seen from the greater perspective, the separation that now exists between recreational, medical, and religious drug use is also unreasonable and the same applies to our perception of drug users. Because we have lost our way so completely as a society, this may not be obvious, but as seen from a principled perspective our schizophrenic view on drug users borders on the comical. Psychiatrist Thomas Szasz noted it thus:

"If the state (official medicine) certifies you as sick and gives you drugs—regardless of whether you need them or not, whether they help you or not, even whether you want them or not—then you are a patient receiving treatment; but if you buy your own drugs and take them on your own initiative—because you feel you need them or, worse, because you want to give yourself peace of mind or pleasure—then you are an addict engaged in drug abuse.

This outlook on life and the policy it engenders rests on a medical imagery that idolizes the therapeutic state as benevolent doctor, and demonizes the autonomous

According to these findings, psychological growth moves towards the FC-end, while psychological pathology is found at the NC-end. See MIKALSEN, *TO RIGHT A WRONG* (2016)

[201] SCHALER (ED.), *DRUGS: SHOULD WE LEGALIZE, DECRIMINALIZE OR DEREGULATE?* (1998) 181

individual as a person who is both a criminal and a patient and whose sole aim in life is to be high on drugs and low on economic productivity."[202]

Because this passage aptly summarizes our view on drug taking, we could easily have solved the "drug problem" by giving all drug users a diagnosis and "medicating" them with their drugs of choice.

This, however, is not the point. The problem goes deeper, and it is not so much that a minority of the drug using population will develop a dysfunctional relationship to their favorite drugs but that we refuse to see them as autonomous agents. In doing so we enable them, for only to the extent that problem-users are perceived as responsible for their lives will they be empowered to change their ways. It is unfortunate therefore that, instead of ascribing responsibility where it is due, we make the mistake of attributing to the drugs some sinister influence. In changing focus from the autonomous agent to an inanimate object, not only do we increase the likelihood that irresponsible drug relationships will evolve but we nourish an unwholesome enemy image. There will always be users who are eager to buy into the notion that drugs have ruined their lives, and as our society encourages this rejection of responsibility, fuel is provided for the myth that drugs are "bad."

I say "myth" as it should be obvious that drugs cannot be "bad," any more than knives or axes can be. It all depends on the user, and just as knives and axes can be used for bad as well as good things, so can drugs. In this sense, a fear of drugs is as irrational as a fear of knives or axes. Their ordinary

---

[202] Sweet & Harris, *Moral and Constitutional Considerations in Support of the Decriminalization of Drugs*, in FISH (ED.), *HOW TO LEGALIZE DRUGS* (1998) 434

intended purpose is benign and at least 90 percent of all use conforms to this norm. Furthermore, drug taking is volitional and there is no need for "pushers" to push them on to anyone. In fact, drug consumers are exactly like other consumers, and the War on Drugs, as Professor Wisotsky has noted, is actually "a war on the American people—their values, needs, and choices, freely expressed in the marketplace of consumer goods."[203]

When it comes to merchandise such as alcohol, tobacco, coffee, and coca cola, this is all too obvious. But when it comes to the illicit drugs prohibitionists turn this logic on its head. Instead of seeing drug users as autonomous agents, they are perceived as being victims of a plague and it becomes their perceived duty to protect people from themselves. This is where prohibitionists' logic breaks down and they leave reason behind. They will apply two wholly different standards to the world; one for the illicit drug users and one for everyone else; and being caught in the grips of the enemy image, they will not question this differently applied logic nor come to terms with its implications. Instead, they will operate on autopilot, ignoring all evidence of cognitive discord and duplicity. Refusing to see the disconnect that gives meaning to their ideology they will eagerly embrace a schizophrenic worldview. They will happily feed and nourish the deception that validates their position, and we shall now see the result of this phenomenon.

---

[203] WISOTSKY, *BEYOND THE WAR ON DRUGS* (1990) 198

2.5.3.1. Different Measures of Harm, Culpability, and Human Dignity

That we are dealing with two different mindsets is evident everywhere, not least in the workings of the U.S. Supreme Court. As Justice Black described the problem of illicit drugs:

> "Commercial traffic in deadly mind-, soul-, and body-destroying drugs is beyond doubt one of the greatest evils of our time. It cripples intellects, dwarfs bodies, paralyzes the progress of a substantial segment of our society, and frequently makes hopeless and sometimes violent and murderous criminals of persons of all ages who become its victims. Such consequences call for the most vigorous laws to suppress the traffic as well as the most powerful efforts to put these vigorous laws into effect."[204]

Would it be conceivable for the justices to describe the trafficking of alcohol in these terms? I think not. It would be difficult to imagine a Court that would label barkeepers and others involved in the distribution chain of alcohol as dealers "in deadly drugs,"[205] and who would describe a young man who on five occasions had sold a can of beer as a "trafficker in human misery."[206] Such terms are reserved for the traffic in illicit drugs, the drugs that are imagined to have no benefits to society, whose users are victims (but still worthy of

---

[204] *Turner v. United States*, 396 U.S.398 (1970) (Black, J., with whom Douglas, J., joins, dissenting.)

[205] Justice Powell discussing drug dealers in *United States v. Mendenhall*, 446 U.S. 544 (1980) 561-562

[206] *United States v. Markham*, C07.126, 191 F.2d 936 (1951) ("The proof had established five different sales of marihuana cigarettes by the defendant, and we do not think it was prejudicial to refer to him as a trafficker in human misery.")

punishment), and whose distributors are "dealers in death", worthy of the most severe sentences.

These different standards result from an exaggerated enemy image. If not for this, the folly would be self-evident, but there it is; it has already separated the world into two different ways of thinking and this disconnect is seen in the different perceptions of harm, culpability, and human dignity that is applied to the two classes of users. The facts speak for themselves, for would the Supreme Court have declined to consider whether a mandatory lifetime sentence for possession of one beer constituted cruel and unusual punishment? Would it have accepted the premise that a person in possession of one beer were implicitly and partly responsible for all the death, misfortune, and misery that the abuse of alcohol contributed to society?

It is difficult to entertain the idea that they would. Still, that was the position of the Court in *Carmona v. Ward,* when it refused to consider whether two mandatory life sentences, one for possession of an ounce of a substance containing cocaine, and the other for sale of 0.00455 of an ounce of a substance containing cocaine, constituted cruel and unusual punishment.

The different logic that applies to licit and illicit drug users is further exemplified by the Supreme Court in *Hutto v. Davis* and *Harmelin v. Michigan.* In the former, the Court approved of imposing 40 years in prison for the possession of 9 ounces of marijuana, while in the latter a young man in possession of 672 grams of cocaine was sentenced to mandatory life. Would the Court, as it did, have attempted to justify such a sentence for barkeepers on account that "a sentence of life imprisonment without parole, while being the second most severe penalty permitted by law, is not grossly disproportionate to the crime of possessing" 100 bottles of vodka? Would it deride his defense by claiming that the "defendant's suggestion that the crime was nonviolent and victimless is false to the point of absurdity"? Would it justify this life sentence by reference to studies that demonstrate the grave threat that alcohol, and particularly strong drink, pose to society in terms of violence, crime, and social displacement?[207]

Again, I think not. While the disastrous consequences of alcohol abuse are factually accurate, it would be difficult to imagine a court which put the responsibility for a minority of alcohol drinkers' excessive use and poor lifestyle choices on the bartender. Still, the Court does not hesitate in comparing Harmelin's crime of possessing 672 grams of cocaine to that of first-degree murder. As Justice Kennedy said: "a rational basis exists . . . to conclude that petitioner's crime is as serious and violent as the crime of felony murder without specific intent to kill,[208] a crime for which no sentence of imprisonment would be disproportionate. . . . A professional seller of addictive drugs may inflict greater bodily harm upon members of society than the person who commits a single assault."[209]

More of the different set of reasoning that is applied in drug cases was seen when Kennedy discussed the connection between crime and drugs. As he said:

---

[207] *Harmelin v. Michigan*, 501 U.S. 957 (1991)

[208] "Felony murder" means that the malicious intent inherent in the commission of any crime, however trivial, is considered to apply to any consequences of that crime, however unintended. As of 2008, 46 states in the United States had a felony murder rule, under which felony murder is generally first-degree murder.

[209] Id.

"Petitioner's suggestion that his crime was nonviolent and victimless . . . is false to the point of absurdity. To the contrary, petitioner's crime threatened to cause grave harm to society.

Quite apart from the pernicious effects on the individual who consumes illegal drugs, such drugs relate to crime in at least three ways: (1) A drug user may commit crime because of drug-induced changes in physiological functions, cognitive ability, and mood; (2) A drug user may commit crime in order to obtain money to buy drugs; and (3) A violent crime may occur as part of the drug business or culture. Studies bear out these possibilities, and demonstrate a direct nexus between illegal drugs and crimes of violence. To mention but a few examples, 57 percent of a national sample of males arrested in 1989 for homicide tested positive for illegal drugs. The comparable statistics for assault, robbery, and weapons arrests were 55, 73 and 63 percent, respectively. In Detroit, Michigan in 1988, 68 percent of a sample of male arrestees and 81 percent of a sample of female arrestees tested positive for illegal drugs. Fifty-one percent of males and seventy-one percent of females tested positive for cocaine. And last year an estimated 60 percent of the homicides in Detroit were drug-related, primarily cocaine-related. *"[210]*

Again, the exact same reasoning could be applied to alcohol and tobacco. A statistically significant percentage of those who come into contact with the criminal justice system will be users of these drugs and while tobacco is no more

---

[210] Id. (Kennedy J., with whom O'Connor J., and Souter J., joins) (sources omitted)

associated with killing sprees than cannabis, alcohol most certainly is.[211]

Furthermore, it bears emphasis that none of these statistics prove a causal connection between drug use and crime. Scholars have found no such link[212] and most of the problems Kennedy addresses are in fact attributable to prohibition, not the pharmacological properties of drugs. Professor Steven Duke speaks to it thus:

> "Contrary to what our government told us when it imposed drug prohibition, most illegal recreational drugs have no pharmacological properties that produce violence or other criminal behavior. Heroin and marijuana diminish rather than increase aggressive behavior. Cocaine—or cocaine withdrawal—occasionally triggers violence but usually does not. Very little crime is generated by the mere use of these drugs, especially in comparison to alcohol, which is causally related to thousands of homicides and hundreds of thousands of

---

[211] BAKALAR & GRINSPOON, *DRUG CONTROL IN A FREE SOCIETY* (1998) 131 ("Half of all wife abusers in Great Britain are heavy drinkers; more than half of the prisoners have serious drinking problems; half of the homicides are committed by people who have been drinking.")

[212] "Independent researchers say that the causal relationship between drugs and crime is merely a hypothesis that has not been proven true. Two scholars from the Earl Warren Legal Institute of the University of California at Berkeley, Franklin Zimring and Gordon Hawkins, who have published a highly regarded study of drug control problems in 1995, even contend that it is untrue. Indeed, they argue that while 'it is beyond dispute that drug use and crime overlap and interact in a multiplicity of ways,' the higher rate of drug use among offenders could be explained by factors in their personality, such as a higher propensity for taking risks and 'a willingness to ignore the threat of moral condemnation,' that lead them to both commit crimes and take drugs. In this view, both drugs and crime are simultaneous but independent consequences of other variables; in simple terms: it is not drug use that causes crime but rather other factors that lead the vast majority of those who commit crime to also take drugs." Laniel, *The Relationship between Research and Drug Policy in the United States* (1999); see also MILLER, *DRUG WARRIORS AND THEIR PREY* (1996) 16-17

assaults annually. The major linkages between illegal drugs and crime must be found elsewhere—in prohibition. . . . [In fact,] the drug war as it is currently being waged probably produces at least half of our serious crime. That is, half of our crime (not counting drug crimes, of course) simply would not occur were we not conducting a drug war. No more damning an indictment of our political leaders can be imagined than that they have affirmatively created half the crime under which we suffer."[213]

The mythical link between crime and drugs was dispelled half a century ago.[214] However, it is a central tenet of prohibitionist reasoning and crops up again and again. A curious example is provided by Justice Boyd of the Florida Supreme Court. The litigant had argued that because *Stanley* protected the private possession of obscene materials, so also the smoking of marijuana in the home should be constitutionally protected. On behalf of the majority, Boyd responded:

---

[213] Duke, *Drug Prohibition: An Unnatural Disaster* (1995) 575, 581 (sources omitted.) For more on how and why prohibition generates crime and other negative externalities, see Benson, *The War on Drugs: A Public Bad* (2008) 4-36; Ostrowski, *Answering the Critics of Drug Legalization* (1991) 12-13; Rasmussen and Benson, *Rationalizing Drug Policy under Federalism* (2003) 685-711; Werb et al., *Effect of Drug Law Enforcement on Drug-Related Violence: Evidence from a Scientific Review* (2010). For more on why prohibition is not justified to prevent crime, see HUSAK, LEGALIZE THIS! (2002) 82-93 and BAKALAR & GRINSPOON, DRUG CONTROL IN A FREE SOCIETY (1998) 133. For other scholars who have pointed out that most drug related deaths and problems are in fact prohibition related, see Barrios & Curtis, *The Impact of the War on Drugs on Puerto Ricans: A Lost Generation*, in FISH (ED.), HOW TO LEGALIZE DRUGS (1998) 125; Majoor, *Drug Policy in the Netherlands: Waiting for a Change*, in FISH (ED.), HOW TO LEGALIZE DRUGS (1998) 152-53

[214] See for instance Bonnie & Whitebread, *The Forbidden Fruit and the Tree of Knowledge* (1970) 1105; KAPLAN, MARIJUANA: THE NEW PROHIBITION (1971)

"Reprehensible as the possession of obscene material may be, the possession and use of marijuana poses a much greater potential threat to society. Appellant states that the primary purpose of smoking marijuana is the 'psychological reaction' it produces in the user and that by smoking marijuana he was 'merely asserting the right to satisfy his intellectual and emotional needs in the privacy of his own home.' This Court is aware that commission of other types of crime, particularly violent crimes, has an emotional effect on the perpetrator. This, however, does not give a constitutional right to commit the crime.

Marijuana does not enjoy the protection of the First Amendment. Its use does not constitute 'private consumption of ideas or information.' Neither are Fourteenth Amendment rights abridged nor the right of privacy violated. Marijuana is a harmful, mind-altering drug. An individual might restrict his possession of marijuana to the privacy of his home, but the effects of the drug are not so restricted. The interest of the state in preventing harm to the individual and to the public at large amply justifies the outlawing of marijuana, in private and elsewhere.

Recently . . . [we recognized] that 'it is to the interest of the state to have strong, robust, healthy citizens, capable of self-support, of bearing arms, and of adding to the resources of the country.' Since marijuana, in addition to harming the individual, is a threat to society as a whole, we have no difficulty in upholding its prohibition by the state."[215]

---

[215] *Borras v. State*, 229 So. 2d 244 (1969) 246

We see how the court describes the high of a marijuana cigarette as comparable to the high of violent crimes, and with this image in mind it is easy to understand why marijuana users are denied constitutional protection. That marijuana users directly harm no one (except themselves) and that the law itself poses a much greater threat to users and society is completely ignored. Ignored is also that the justices' fundamental premise—the premise that the government has a right to take whatever measures it deems fit in its battle against imagined social problems—is inherently flawed. Reasoning by analogy the court could just as well have compared the high of runners, chocolate eaters, coca cola drinkers, and tobacco smokers with the psychopathic high of the violent offender, and on this basis justified the criminalization of such individuals.

The Florida Supreme Court, however, does not merely grant the government full authority to deal with perceived evils; it takes its reasoning to its logical conclusion, and by implication extends to the government a right to healthy citizens.

The government, of course, has no such right. Only in totalitarian states like Hitler's Germany do the state have an imagined right to citizens who are "strong, robust, healthy, capable of self-support, of bearing arms, and of adding to the resources of the country." The idea belongs to the extreme totalitarian-end, and the founders' America is the very antithesis to this notion. As Professor Fuller pointed out 50 years ago, *the essence of the modern state project is the distinction between a morality of duty and a morality of aspiration.* The morality of duty concerns our duties to our fellowmen: We shall, in short, not infringe on each other's autonomy or liberty rights, and the state is there to ensure that we do not violate the rights of other persons. The morality of duty, then, concerns *the very least* that we can expect from each other; it sets the bar where we cannot lower it further, not without unduly infringing the rights of others to the same liberties as ourselves. This threshold equals the parameter of justice. Not only can it not be lowered; it cannot be heightened, as the idea of freedom would become meaningless.

In other words, it is *only* if we fail to live up to the morality of duty as it is defined by this threshold that the state may rightfully intervene. *Any unwanted state meddling in our private affairs must be because we have failed to abide by the morality of duty*, and while we can all do better—be more compassionate, altruistic, and service-oriented—the state has no right to expect this from us. This is where the morality of aspiration kicks in, and it is entirely up to the individual to figure out how he/she will honor his/her higher aspirations. Drug users therefore cannot be expected to conform to any other standard than the morality of duty. However, if they fail to do so, there are already laws to deal with those misbehaviors that affect the rights of others and the drug law cannot be justified on such grounds. It is merely another testimony to the different standards we apply to drug users that the Florida Court would embrace such reasoning. For as Husak noted, "[a]part from the context of drug use, no one believes that anyone possesses a right to mandate that persons be healthy, that workers be productive, that parents be good, that neighbors be reliable, or that students be attentive."[216] If this were the case, most of how we organize our lives would

---

[216] Husak, *Two Rationales for Drug Policy* in FISH (ED.), *HOW TO LEGALIZE DRUGS* (1998) 52

be subject to restrictions and the idea of liberty would be void of all content.

Another area where we see the application of the different standards is in those courts where the criterion for upholding the prohibition is whether marijuana is a harmless drug. Several courts have ruled in favor of the state because the appellant has not succeeded in convincing the judges that marijuana is a completely harmless substance.[217] In doing so, they are misframing the issue, for the question is not whether marijuana is a harmless recreational drug. The question is whether the possible harms are significant enough to merit prohibition; whether prohibition is the least intrusive means available; whether prohibition is suited to deal with the alleged harms; and whether the harms associated with the drug are less significant than the harms attributed to prohibition.[218]

Furthermore, we see the different standards being applied on the eagerness with which the courts defer to the legislature because of the "unknown" harms associated with illicit drugs. The argument is that "alcohol is susceptible to a less restrictive alternative means of control," because "there are recognized, accurate means of determining its use and its abuse" and "the effects of alcohol upon the user are

---

[217] *Commonwealth v. Leis,* 355 Mass. 189, 243 N.E.2d 898 (1969); *Marcoux v. Attorney General,* 375 Mass. 63, (1978); *United States v. Maas,* 551 F. Supp. 645 (D.N.J. 1982) 648 ("Defendants could not prove that it has been established conclusively that use of marijuana is harmless, yet only such proof could alter this court's determination that the legislation is supported by a rational justification.")

[218] As Justice Abe of the Hawaii Supreme Court stated "the finding that marijuana is harmful to the user does not authorize the State under its police power to prohibit its use under threat of punishment. Under the doctrine . . . the State must prove that the use of marijuana is not only harmful to the user but also to the general public before it can prohibit its use." *State v. Kantner,* 493 P.2d 306 (1972) at 313 (Abe J., concurring)

known."[219] However, these are not viable reasons for imprisoning drug users. As Justice Seiler of the Missouri Supreme Court noted:

> "This contention is unresponsive for two reasons. The first is that however 'incomplete' our knowledge may be or how 'debatable' the 'medical issue' concerning marijuana may be or how much 'dis-agreement or controversy' may surround any discussion concerning the drug, this grants no legislative license to violate one's constitutional right to be free from cruel and unusual punishment. There is surely less 'debate' and 'controversy' concerning the assuredly harmful effects of cigarette smoking. Yet were the legislature to prohibit the sale of cigarettes as a crime, I question whether this court would be as deferential were the legislature to mandate a penalty of imprisonment from five years to life for the sale of less than half a pack.
>
> The second reason [why this] view is unresponsive is that [the court] has shielded itself behind alleged factual uncertainty which is the relic of an earlier day. No longer can we realistically claim, as once we could, that the data upon which to judge the effects of marijuana is either unreliable, crudely assembled, or considerably outdated. Substantial private research . . . has been joined by . . . comprehensive government supported efforts, well-financed studies utilizing advanced scientific analysis. These studies demonstrably, effectively, categorically, and reliably show that there is no firm evidence that marijuana as presently used in this country is attended with danger to the user or to others."[220]

---

[219] *Leis 355 Mass.* 189 (1969) 198

[220] *State v. Michell*, 563 S.W.2d 18 (1978) 29-30 (Seiler, J., dissenting)

Regarding Seiler's first point, the different measures of human dignity attributed to tobacco and cannabis smokers and the different measure of harm we attach to the products, it is made evident in *RJR-MacDonald Inc.*, where the Canadian Supreme Court investigated the possibility of prohibiting tobacco. Despite the Court's finding that "the detrimental health effects of tobacco consumption are both dramatic and substantial," the Court held that the government was justified in not criminalizing tobacco consumption. The reason for this decision was that criminalizing tobacco products "would likely lead many smokers to resort to alternative, and illegal, sources of supply," rendering such an approach "unfeasible."[221]

Now again, the exact same thing can be said of the criminalization of other drugs and the only relevant difference is that the potential harms associated with cannabis consumption pale in comparison to the harms caused by tobacco consumption. Why, then, do our officials come to opposite conclusions? Why is prohibition a valid endeavor when it comes to one type of drugs but not the other? How can we reconcile the use of two divergent scales of harm and human dignity?

An answer is yet to be provided.

2.5.3.2. Different Measures of Rationality

When asked to defend their policies, prohibitionists will say that drug use is a disaster to society and that it is not

---

[221] *RJR-MacDonald Inc. v. Canada (Attorney General)*, (1995) 3 S.C.R. 199

compatible with a rational conception of the good life. According to them, drug use is construed as pathological behavior, as an objectionable activity that deserves no recognition, and to legalize drugs would be to "send the wrong message."

As other scholars have noted, however, it is a myth that drug use is necessarily pathological and in reality it is indistinguishable from other pleasure-giving activities such as eating, sex, and falling in love.[222] Even addicts can be said to "have chosen to follow a way of life which offers them the rewards of activity, company and a recognized identity,"[223] and to "single out drug use as necessarily and uniquely harmful to reason (and so specifically worthy of prohibition) is to fall for the 'myth of the demon drugs.'"[224]

If we are to paint drug use as an irrational activity, a habit that no sound mind would pursue, we must adopt Jon Elster's definition of rational choice which involves three optimizations: Optimization of action, given desires and beliefs; optimization of beliefs, given the available information; and optimization of information acquisition given desires and beliefs.[225]

Using this standard, we can see that some types of drug use (but not all) could be defined as irrational behavior. But then again, so would the behaviors of the rest of the population. It is all a matter of perspective, and as seen from

---

[222] Fingarette, *Addiction and Criminal Responsibility* in SCHALER (ED.), *DRUGS: SHOULD WE LEGALIZE, DECRIMINALIZE OR DEREGULATE?* (1998) 306-38; DE GREIFF (ED.), *DRUGS AND THE LIMITS OF LIBERALISM* (1999) at 46-58, 102-06, 123-27, 144-52; HUSAK, *DRUGS AND RIGHTS* (1996) 81-130

[223] Stevens, *Drug policy, harm and human rights: A rationalist approach* (2011) 235
[224] Ibid.

[225] Elster, *Rationality and Addiction*, in DE GREIFF (ED.), *DRUGS AND THE LIMITS OF LIBERALISM* (1999) 25-45

the FC-end hardly anything we do meets this strict standard of rationality.[226] The footnote provides us with a few examples, and when it comes to prohibitionists it is well known that they themselves demonstrate the exact same traits as are associated with the most hardcore drug addicts.[227] The history of drug prohibition, after all, is a history of the extent to which they have denied reality in order to feed an oppressive habit and mistaken sense of moral superiority. And if their irrational behavior is not already apparent, consider this: If disagreement helps us rethink our position, sharpen our intellect, improve our analysis, and see past our own misconceptions, why are prohibitionists not willing to debate the pros and cons of current drug policies? If

---

[226] Let us begin here: If we seek a better world, why are we slowly destroying the planet? Considering the evidence to suggest that the inner and outer world are not separate entities; that our thoughts do have an impact on our surroundings; and that those thoughts that follow from the Wholeness perspective (the psychology of love) create harmony, while those thoughts that are derived from the idea of separation (the psychology of fear) generate all our troubles: Why do we not make a conscious and consistent effort to embrace those thoughts that follow from the position of love? If we want to live happy lives and if we want a better future for our children, why do we choose those thoughts and actions that generate discord rather than harmony? Considering that research from the social sciences indicate that people who live in equality-oriented, freedom-oriented, and collaborative-oriented societies live happier, healthier, and more peaceful lives, why do we choose the opposite? Why do we choose hierarchical, control-oriented, and competition-oriented societies? And not least: Considering that the only sound measure of the integrity among politicians is the extent to which they support human rights—and considering that most of them, in action if not words, show a contempt for these rights in the management of our affairs—why do we elect them? Why are they not held to account for the devious wars and double dealings in which they indulge? Why do we let young men and women fight wars of aggression? Why do we time and time again fall victim to our officials' lies and misdirection?

[227] Barnett, *Bad Trip* (1994) 2598 ("It seems that no facts are sufficient to shake the prohibitionists' faith in this tragic policy. As . . . suggested elsewhere, some persons act as though they are addicted to drug laws, with all the connotations of irrationality that term is meant to convey when applied to drug users. Consequently, they are unlikely to be swayed by the copious facts and arguments presented [by reform activists]. . . . [Nonetheless] the case against prohibition is overwhelming, precisely because so many different types of considerations all point to a single solution: the legalization of illicit drugs.")

prohibitionists really want what is best for humanity, why are they unwilling to let these policies be reviewed by an independent, impartial, and competent tribunal?

No one of sound mind would dedicate themselves to a position like this and then refuse to consider if the position is at all defensible—and yet, this is what prohibitionists have done. Hence, they are throwing stones in glass houses whenever they try to paint drug use as an irrational pursuit, and as 90 percent of drug use does not even fit the DSM-IV diagnostic criteria for dependence, we have no reason to regard drug use as an irrational endeavor.

This being so, the courts' willingness to accept the criminalization of drugs due to the legislature's fear of "sending the wrong signal" is misplaced. First of all, as Judge Sweet and Harris pointed out, "the moral question of what laws a government ought to enact and enforce is logically independent of what the individual ought to do."[228] As such, a move away from prohibition does not mean that politicians approve of drug use; it just means that they recognize that there are areas of the individual domain where they have no business interfering—that's all. Secondly, the message politicians really are sending is not a message that we should listen to. As Sheriff Bill Masters wryly noted:

"If you want to know the "message" politicians are sending to our children with the drug war, here it is: it's okay for armed enforcers to kill innocent children . . . if they believe drugs to be present. It's okay for police to bust down doors in the middle of the night with submachine guns locked and loaded, if some drugged-up,

---

[228] Sweet & Harris, *Moral and Constitutional Considerations in Support of the Decriminalization of Drugs*, IN FISH (ED.), *HOW TO LEGALIZE DRUGS* (1998) 447

paid informant said there might be drugs around. It's okay for police to take your property without even charging you with a crime. It's okay for politicians to wipe their feet on the Bill of Rights, as long as they are doing it in the name of getting tough on drug dealers. That's the 'morality' of the War on Drugs."[229]

This is, of course, no true morality. The world of ethics that has spawned a War on Drugs is increasingly being seen for what it is, but prohibitionists have yet to recognize their error.

2.5.3.3. Different Measures of Weight

Another area where we see the absurdity of prohibition unfold is in the measurement of drugs before trial. In *Chapman* the Supreme Court held that the punishment for LSD possession should be meted out based on the weight of the carrier medium and not the potency of the substance.[230] This logic also applies to other illicit drugs: "Drugs are drugs" and the punishment is the same whether or not they are of poor or superior quality. By the same logic, possession of a gallon of water containing 0.1 percent alcohol should be met with the same criminal sanction as possession of a gallon containing 98 percent alcohol.

However, while it is unlikely that the Court would have failed to treat the two gallons of alcohol differently, the lack of reason that is attached to drug cases is even more profound.

---

[229] MASTERS, *DRUG WAR ADDICTION* (2001) 61

[230] LSD is a substance whose dosages are measured in micrograms and pure LSD is usually dissolved in alcohol. Droplets containing LSD crystals are normally applied to a carrier medium like blotter paper or sugar cubes.

For instance, in *Fowner*,[231] a man who had been arrested in possession of 79.7 grams of methamphetamine was also charged—*and convicted*—for being in possession of approximately 24 gallons of a liquid mixture containing detectable amounts of a controlled substance. At trial, an expert testified that the liquid was a waste byproduct of methamphetamine manufacturing and that it was an uningestable waste. Still, the Court of Appeals held that so long as the liquid contained a detectable amount of a controlled substance, its entire weight was properly included in the calculation of the defendant's sentence under the Guidelines.

The Supreme Court accepted this decision.[232]

2.5.3.4. Different Measures of Bodily Autonomy

Another area which shows the different logic that applies to drug users is the different measures of harm and human dignity that is utilized in abortion cases and drug cases.

Whether or not a fetus counts as a "person," it at least represents a potential human life, and that potential life is extinguished by abortion. A prohibition on abortion therefore protects the life or potential life of human beings. In other words, important rights are at stake, but with *Planned Parenthood v. Casey* the Court determined that a woman's right to bodily autonomy was so fundamental that neither the

---

[231] *Fowner v. U. S.*, 112 S. Ct. 1998, 118 L. Ed. 2d 594, 60 U.S.L.W. 3778 (1992)

[232] Judge Posner called such judgments "loony," pointing out that "to base punishments on the weight of the carrier medium makes about as much sense as basing punishment on the weight of the defendant." BOWARD, *LOST RIGHTS* (1995) 210

state nor her husband had a right to interfere with her "interest in deciding whether to bear and beget a child."[233]

There can be no doubt that a woman's decision to have an abortion may have a profound impact on others. Society, not to mention her spouse, family, and unborn child all have an obvious interest at stake, and yet her right to bodily autonomy overrides any other concern. If this is so, it is difficult to see why drug users are denied the same right to bodily autonomy. No doubt they, like alcohol drinkers, may make poor lifestyle decisions and no doubt they may suffer for it, but no good reasons have been given for treating drug users' right to bodily autonomy any differently.[234]

2.5.3.5. Different Standards for Evaluating Bodily Integrity

In *Washington v. Harper* the Supreme Court "had no doubt" that "a significant liberty interest" was at stake and used heightened review to decide whether the state could administer antipsychotic drugs to a prisoner against his will. Justice Stevens held that:

---

[233] *Casey*, 505 U.S. at 858-59

[234] Relying on *Roe v. Wade* and *Casey*, two abortion cases wherein the Supreme Court majority credited the state's interest to preserve the life of the fetus as 'important' but nevertheless insufficient to prohibit the practice when measured against the liberty interests of the mother, Justice Seeley of the Washington Supreme Court held that the drug laws were unconstitutional. As he said: "The majority cannot distinguish these cases. If the state cannot prohibit abortions consistent with due process, it can hardly constitutionally prohibit drug use as its interest to do so is arguably much less important." *Seeley v. State*, 132 Wash. 2d 776, 940 P.2d 604 (1997) 623 (Sanders J., dissenting)

"Every violation of a person's bodily integrity is an invasion of his or her liberty. . . . Moreover, any such action is degrading if it overrides a competent person's choice to reject a specific form of medical treatment. And when the purpose or effect of forced drugging is to alter the will and the mind of the subject, it constitutes a deprivation of liberty in the most literal and fundamental sense. . . . The liberty of citizens to resist the administration of mind-altering drugs arises from our Nation's most basic values."[235]

The concern were prisoners' autonomy rights and Justice Stevens defended the right not to be forcibly administered psychotropic drugs. However, speaking in terms of autonomy, it is no less a violation of mental and bodily integrity to be deprived of a choice than to have it forced upon us. Even though the latter is likely to be regarded as a more intrusive violation, the denial of free will is equally present, and there can be no denying that the encroachment of choice itself constitutes a violation of mental/bodily integrity.

Prohibitionists, for their part, have great difficulty in seeing how this is so as they consider drug prohibition to be in everybody's best interest. Nonetheless, we must not forget that drug prohibition itself represents an attempt "to alter the will and the mind of the subject" by the administration of force. *No doubt* also this is experienced by many millions of Americans as an invasion of their liberty, and *no doubt* also this is experienced as a degrading deprivation of autonomy— one that in many cases has even more serious consequences than being force-fed "medication." Consequently, while philosophers may argue whether one or the other constitutes

---

[235] *Washington v. Harper*, 494 U.S. 210 (1990) 239 (Stevens J., dissenting)

a worse deprivation of autonomy, no one can seriously dispute that both "constitute a deprivation of liberty in the most literal and fundamental sense;" that the same liberty interests are involved whether one is being forcibly deprived of choice or whether one is being forcibly imposed a choice; and that the liberty to be free from both impositions "arises from our Nation's most basic values."

The real issue, then, is in both cases if the government interest is sufficient to overcome an individual's autonomy rights. As we have seen, this issue has yet to be determined by an impartial, independent, and competent court. Nonetheless, as the Washington Supreme Court and other courts have concluded that "a competent individual's right to refuse such medication is a fundamental liberty interest deserving the highest order of protection,"[236] one may wonder what objective reasons the courts can find for denying the same protection to competent individuals being forcibly deprived of their choice in drugs.

2.5.3.6. Meaningless Models of Blameworthiness

We have already noted the different measures of culpability that attach to licit and illicit drug users. When it comes to the former, responsibility is put where responsibility is due—that is with the individual for those actions and lifestyle choices he himself chooses to pursue. The latter is not so fortunate, and with *Rodriguez*[237] we are provided with another example of the injustice that drug users must suffer.

---

[236] Id.

[237] *New Jersey v. Rodriguez*, 645 A.2d 1165 (1994)

In this case, Carlos Rodriguez was sentenced to 18 years for the murder of Susan Hendricks and Fred Bennett. The situation that led to his conviction was the following: Bennett and Hendricks arrived at Rodriguez's apartment to buy cocaine. Immediately after their purchase, the police raided the premises and to avoid persecution Bennett and Hendricks swallowed the cocaine. As a result, they both died and Rodriguez was charged with first degree murder.[238]

This is the logic of prohibition in a nutshell. These deaths were clearly the result of drug policy, but prohibitionists refuse to face reality and blame the victims. Both these deaths, therefore, were listed as overdose deaths and used by the government as examples of the threat that drugs pose to society. Rodriguez, for his part, challenged his conviction, claiming that it constituted cruel and unusual punishment and violated the Eighth Amendment, but the U.S. Supreme Court would not hear of it. We have already seen drug users' liberty or autonomy interests count for naught. And because the drug law, as far as the Court is concerned, does not touch upon important interests, all that is needed is a rational basis. Hence, because the law, in the eyes of prohibitionists, passes this test the Court saw no reason to intervene.

Even so, that the same logic applied to car manufacturers would have survived the rational basis test should have been a warning to the justices that something was amiss. One would clearly expect General Motors to make safer cars if they were held personally accountable for all traffic-related

---

[238] The Comprehensive Drug Reform Act of 1986 holds that "any person who manufactures, distributes, or dispenses . . . any . . . controlled dangerous substance classified in Schedule I or II . . . is liable for a death which results from the injection, inhalation, or ingestion of that substance, and is guilty of a crime of the first degree." At least 14 states impose strict liability for such deaths and two even have capital punishment for those convicted of the crime.

deaths, including those resulting from bad government policies, but no sane person would hold such a statute to be a rational application of law. The question, obviously, is not if the law is "rationally related" to some government purpose, but if it is morally related to the nature of the offense. For punishment to be just, it must be proportional to the moral culpability of the offender, and if the concept of blameworthiness is to have any meaning, Rodriguez cannot be blamed for these deaths.

Prohibitionists may think that he got what he deserved but it should be unnecessary to remind them that the same logic applied to alcohol, tobacco, and pharmaceutical drugs would result in imprisonment for life of almost every truck driver, shop clerk, doctor, and bartender in America, along with millions of regular citizens. In fact, by consistently (and more appropriately) applying this logic, one is tempted to ask these justices what punishment they would mete out to the engineers of war. What sort of sentences would be appropriate for the producers of war material, to those who profit from it, and to all those soldiers who do battle? And last but not least, what sort of penalties would be proper for politicians, those pathological liars who have a record of supporting any war, no matter its merits, to satisfy the expectations of war-profiteers?

In all these cases, objectively speaking, punishment would be much more appropriate as *every single one* of them—and to a much greater extent—are morally blameworthy for their actions. I mean, speaking of drug producers, traffickers, and dealers, those in the receiving end of their trade are eager to accept their products; at the very least 90 percent of their consumers use their products responsibly and even the latter 10 percent are thankful. Who can say this about producers of war material and those that put such products to use? How many in the receiving end of a missile, bomb, grenade, or bullet appreciate their contribution to the world?

Anyone with their moral sensibilities intact understands that war profiteers have a personal responsibility for the misfortunes of humanity that extends far beyond that of drug dealers.[239] Morally, it is not even the same ballgame; we are talking the difference between night and day—unless, of course, the prohibitionists can show us that drugs really destroy the mind, rendering users incapable of autonomous choice.

Only the undue influence of the collective unconscious may make this comparison unheard-of. To the extent that we are in its grip, we will equal state action with morality, and our moral code will be turned upside down. As discussed in *To Right a Wrong*, FC ideals and values will have to become NC values and vice versa, and the result is a collective psychosis where our moral compass is obliterated. This is the price we must pay for conforming to the status quo. We simply cannot afford to put two and two together because it would lay bare the profound immorality of state action. Hence, to overcome truth and to preserve the delusion, "all

---

[239] To sleep at night, war profiteers imagine that they are involved in an industry which purpose is to protect society from harm. In their mind, their contribution is to those so-called "just" wars, and their moral compass is guided by the supposition that any government sanctioned activity must be moral. Such naïve thinking do not merit an elaborate response; suffice to say that *no war* the Western powers have fought the last 60 years satisfies the "just war" defense, that any belief to the contrary mirrors a profound unawareness of power-politics, and that this childish, unthinking notion only survives insofar as people are unaware of the propaganda apparatus that is in place to keep their consciousness focused on the surface of events—a surface that is constantly being polished by lies and misdirection. For more on this, see MIKALSEN, *REASON IS* (2014)

that is needed," to paraphrase Orwell, "is an unending series of victories over our own reason."

Nowhere is this better seen than in drug policy. It is only because of the influence of an enemy image that the injustice of subjecting drug law violators to prohibitionist reasoning is not immediately obvious. Had we thought about things, we would have understood that it being *exactly the same* supply and demand mechanisms involved when it comes to the two classes of drugs, it is clear that drug distributors like Rodriguez are in fact no eviller and more depraved than anyone involved with the supply-chain of alcohol and tobacco.

Accepting this, the next logical step would be to come to grips with its implications—that the drug law enforcers, in fact, are worse than the drug dealers. From a constitutional perspective, the latter have merely provided people with a service they want, while the drug law enforcers have done so much worse. In their enforcement of these laws they have tapped people's phones, opened their mail, spied on them, searched their houses, stripped them naked, performed cavity searches, fined them, demonised them, discriminated against them, stigmatised them, terrorised them, confiscated and destroyed their property and valuables, forced them into "rehabilitation," jailed them, taken their children, destroyed their education and work possibilities, threatened them, humiliated them, beaten them, shot at them, and even killed them. And what is worse, on those occasions when the victims have opposed such abusive behaviours and sought to set things straight in accordance with human rights law, these enforcers—to preserve their pretensions of personal virtue— have denied them every opportunity to meaningfully challenge the law.

As we have seen, under no circumstances can the purveyors of the status quo bear to face reality. It would be too crushing to their self-esteem, and so we continue to live in a society in which each state undertakes to respect and ensure to all individuals—except the drug law violators—the rights recognised in the Constitution; where all persons, except them, shall be equal before the law and be entitled to equal protection of the law; where everybody, except them, shall be recognised as a person before the courts and entitled to a fair hearing by a competent, impartial and independent tribunal to have their rights determined; where everybody, except them, shall have an effective remedy against unlawful detention as well as abusive, discriminatory and degrading policies; and where everyone, except them, shall have an enforceable right to compensation after being the victim of such practices.

We live in a society in which everybody, except them, shall have the right to self-determination and to freely pursue their social, cultural, economic and spiritual development; where every human being, except them, shall have the inherent right to life and to be protected from being arbitrarily deprived of it; where no one, except the drug law violators, shall be subjected to cruel, inhuman or degrading treatment or punishment; where no one, but them, shall be subjected to arbitrary and unlawful interference with his privacy, family, home or correspondence, and where everyone, but them, have the right to be protected by law against such interferences.

We are supposed to accept a social contract where everyone, except them, have the right to liberty and security of person, and where no one, but them, shall be unlawfully deprived of their liberty; where everyone, but them, shall have the right to freedom of expression and to seek, collect and impart information and ideas of all kinds, regardless of frontiers; where any propaganda for war—except drug war—shall be prohibited by law; where any advocacy of hatred that constitutes incitement to discrimination, hostility or violence shall be prohibited by law—except that which is directed at the drug law violators; and where any family, except theirs, are entitled to protection by society and the state.

These, I am sure, may be tough words for prohibitionists to hear. In their minds, they have sought to rid the world of a terrible plague. They have been soldiers in a crusade that was to be for the betterment of Mankind, and it is difficult to readjust this frame of reference into one more conforming to reality. However, if they wonder whether they are on the side of good, they need only ask drug users whose services they prefer: Do they favour the dealers, those who respect their autonomous choice, or the drug law enforcers, those who infantilize and persecute them?

Prohibitionists should not be surprised to find that the drug users, like alcohol drinkers, tobacco smokers, or chocolate eaters, greatly prefer to interact with that group who cater to their will rather than that group who, by the whims of their own self-asserted authority, threaten them with imprisonment to save them from themselves.

This being so, unless prohibitionists can put forth good reasons why these people have no say in the management of their own affairs, the drug dealers are in fact agents of autonomy. If this is so, it is also clear that the law enforcers must be the agents of tyranny—and that, in matters of blameworthiness, they themselves are much more liable to criminal persecution than violators. Moral culpability, after all, must be the result of a violation of autonomy rights, either in a collective or individual capacity. Because of this thieves, rapists, and murderers are worthy of persecution, but none have shown drug use to violate the rights of others. Instead, as professors of law and philosophy have pointed out, it is drug prohibition that violates autonomy rights,[240] and so—unless prohibitionists can prove this argument wrong—the drug law enforcers are the real "traffickers in human misery."

2.5.3.7. Neglecting the Obvious Implications

No wonder prohibitionists refuse to face reality. Had they been willing to think about things they would, as Miller noted, have understood that "transforming ordinary productive citizens into criminals for conduct having less measurable harm than tolerated conduct, is a sign of religious zealotry rather than public welfare."[241] They would, as Justice Seiler noted, have understood that "[w]hen one generation irrationally uses the criminal sanction to coerce and intimidate another into rejecting a relatively harmless drug, marijuana, while openly promoting the use of what we know to be relatively harmful drugs, alcohol and tobacco, respect

---

[240] Moore, *Liberty and Drugs*, in DE GREIFF (ED.), *DRUGS AND THE LIMITS OF LIBERALISM* (1999) 89 ("our desires, feeling, and beliefs are not our own . . . if they are simply the product of social coercion or mere conforming imitation of social convention: 'He who lets the world . . . choose his life plan for him has no need for any other faculty than the apelike one of imitation.'"); Husak, *Liberal Neutrality, Autonomy, and Drug Prohibitions* (2000) 69-70

[241] MILLER, *THE CASE FOR LEGALIZING DRUGS* (1991) 126. Other scholars have pointed out that drug prohibition is akin to religious persecution. See DUKE & CROSS, *AMERICA'S LONGEST WAR* (1993) 156; SZASZ, *CEREMONIAL CHEMISTRY* (2003); and Ostrowski, *Drug Prohibition Muddles Along*, in FISH (ED.), *HOW TO LEGALIZE DRUGS* (1998) 366. ("The only civilized way to deal with irreconcilable conflicts in ultimate values is to declare freedom of religion and let each go his or her own way. That is the last thing the prohibitionists have in mind. Rather, their solution to the problem of irreconcilable conflict of values over drugs is to inflict on those who disagree with them all the force and violence they can muster.")

for law and the legal process suffers."[242] And they would have seen the parallels between their own crusade and those of earlier days.[243]

The argument presented above is after all exceedingly simple. An unbiased twelve-year old could follow the logic to its conclusion, and so the problem is not a mental incapacity to reflect or understand. The problem is that, psychologically speaking, it is extremely difficult to come to terms with this understanding—and this explains the self-righteous conviction with which the aggressors pursue their prey, as well as the breakdown of logic that always accompanies their reasoning.

We have seen it repeated over and over, and more examples will be provided. We have already discussed the Supreme Court's reasoning in *Harmelin,* where it accepted the constitutionality of mandatory life sentences for those in possession of drugs. The majority opinion was a paragon of prohibitionist reasoning, but the refusal to think about things was also made evident by the dissent. To their credit, White, Blackmun, Marshall, and Stevens acknowledged the erroneous reasoning that the majority used to justify its position and noted the following in their dissent: (1) that "to be constitutionally proportionate, punishment must be tailored to a defendant's personal responsibility and moral guilt;" (2) that "unlike crimes directed against the persons and property of others, possession of drugs affects the criminal who uses the drugs most directly;" (3) that "while the

---

[242] *State v. Mitchell,* 563 S.W.2d 18 (1978) 32 (Seiler J., dissenting, Sp. J., Shangler concurring)

[243] For a comparison with the Inquisition, see SZASZ, CEREMONIAL CHEMISTRY (2003) 61-74. For a comparison with Nazism, see MIKALSEN, REASON IS (2014) 467-81; MILLER, *THE CASE FOR LEGALIZING DRUGS* (1991) 118-24; MILLER, *DRUG WARRIORS AND THEIR PREY* (1996)

collateral consequences of drugs such as cocaine are indisputably severe, they are not unlike those which flow from the misuse of other, legal, substances;" (4) that "it is inconceivable that a State could rationally choose to penalize one who possesses large quantities of alcohol in a manner similar to that in which Michigan has chosen to punish petitioner for cocaine possession, because of the tangential effects which might ultimately be traced to the alcohol at issue;" and (5) that "the ripple effect on society caused by possession of drugs, through related crimes, lost productivity, health problems, and the like, is often not the direct consequence of possession, but of the resulting addiction, something which this Court held in *Robinson* cannot be made a crime."[244]

When it comes to drugs, this is the most lucid thinking we have seen from the Supreme Court. This, unfortunately, is not saying much, as the justices did not follow their reasoning through. Had they taken their own calculations seriously, they would have added these five points together and checked how this line of reasoning correlated with the principles of fundamental justice, but no such effort was made. It is regrettable that they neglected this obvious next step, as they would have had to conclude that the Constitution not only invalidated the appellant's life sentence *but that its principles also laid bare the unconstitutionality of drug prohibition.* They noticed the wholly different logic that is being applied to the two classes of drugs and they recognized "that to be constitutionally proportional, punishment must be tailored to a defendant's personal responsibility and moral guilt."[245]

---

[244] *Harmelin v. Michigan*, 501 U.S. 957 (1991) (White J., dissenting)

[245] The Supreme Court also recognized this principle in *Carmona*, where the appeals court had rationalized petitioners' sentences "by invoking all evils attendant on or

Accepting this, the foundation of drug prohibition is crumbling, as a proper equality and proportionality analysis would have found inconsistencies which could only have been remedied by abolishing the law. First, by applying coherent reasoning, the drug law's shaky foundation (which is the different standards it uses to define and to deal with harms) would have been exposed. And secondly, had they looked at reality, they would have seen that the standard applied to the licit drugs (that of personal responsibility) was what reasonable people would agree on. They would have had to conclude that this standard conformed to the principles of justice, while the one that is being applied to illicit drugs would have been found to be as irrational as the fear that ensured its survival.

In the history of the Court, this was the closest the justices ever got to getting it right. They outlined the bigger picture but failed to connect the dots. This is nothing new, as psychological incentives ensure that prohibitionists can never afford to think their argument through. If they did, its incoherence would have to be recalibrated into one of harmony with reason and the principles of justice, and they prefer the status quo.

In the following, we shall further explore the ingenuity with which meaningful review is kept at bay.

---

attributable to widespread drug trafficking." As the Court held, this "is simply not compatible with a fundamental premise of the criminal justice system, that individuals are accountable only for their own criminal acts." *Carmona et al. v. Ward, Correctional Commissioner, et al.*, 439 U.S. 1091, 99 S. Ct. 874, 59 L. Ed. 2d 58 (1979)

2.5.4. Relying on Prejudice and Flawed Analysis

To support the use of conflicting logic prohibitionists will sometimes try to explain why it is reasonable to treat alcohol drinkers differently than illicit drug users. In this passage from *Commonwealth v. Leis*, the trial judge gives it a shot:

> "The ordinary user of marijuana is quite likely to be a marginally adjusted person who turns to the drug to avoid confrontation with and the resolution of his problems. The majority of alcohol users are well adjusted, productively employed individuals who use alcohol for relaxation and as an incident of other social activities."[246]

The problem is that there is no empirical evidence to support this view. There is only prejudice and ignorance to sustain it but because prohibitionists are never asked to validate the premises of their argument, this type of reasoning persists.

Another example was provided by the Appeals Court, when Judge Spiegel said that:

> "There are at least two distinctions between alcohol and the 'mind altering intoxicants' that are defined by the law to be narcotic drugs. First, alcohol is susceptible to a less restrictive alternative means of control. There are recognized, accurate means of determining its use and its abuse. Second, the effects of alcohol upon the user are known. We think that the Legislature is warranted in treating this known intoxicant differently from

---

[246] Bonnie & Whitebread, *The Forbidden Fruit and the Tree of Knowledge* (1970) 1131

marihuana, LSD or heroin, the effects of which are largely still unknown and subject to extensive dispute."[247]

Whatever merit this argument might have had 50 years ago, it is, as Justice Seiler previously remarked, no good today. Since the *Leis* court, no plant has been more carefully studied than cannabis, and still prohibitionists are arguing that we "just do not know enough" to grant the defendant the benefit of the doubt.

Furthermore, another example was provided by the German Constitutional Court when it said that:

"There are also important reasons for the differing treatment of Cannabis products and alcohol. It is indeed accepted that the *abuse* of alcohol brings with it dangers both for the individual and for society which are equal to or even greater than those posed by Cannabis products. However, it must be borne in mind that alcohol can be used in many ways. There are no comparable uses for the products and parts of the Cannabis plant. Products containing alcohol serve as a source of nourishment and pleasure. In the form of wine they are also used in religious ceremonies. In all cases the dominant use of alcohol does not lead to states of intoxication. Its intoxicating effect is generally known and is generally avoided by means of social controls. In contrast, the achievement of an intoxicated state is usually the main aim when Cannabis products are used. Furthermore the legislature finds itself in the situation that it cannot effectively prevent the consumption of alcohol because

---

[247] *Commonwealth v. Leis*, 355 Mass. 189 (1969) 198

of traditional patterns of consumption in Germany and the European cultural sphere."[248]

Even though this example is from a foreign court, it so perfectly describes the reasoning that is being used to sustain the status quo that it begged for inclusion. Only very rarely will the courts attempt to justify the different treatment of alcohol and cannabis consumers. I have not found other examples from American courtrooms, and the attempts discussed so far should explain why. After all, everything that is said of alcohol can also be said of cannabis, and again we see the court appeal to ignorance rather than reason. To this day, whenever prohibitionists try to enlighten us on the qualitative difference between licit and illicit drugs, this has always been the case. And this being so, it is little wonder that courts usually just defer to the legislature.

Whenever this is done, we find plenty of shoddy reasoning. To divest of the issue, they must look to precedent, and it bears noticing that the courts always refer to irrelevant precedent. To deny appellants their day in court, they will refer to *Lindsley v. Natural Carbonic Gas,*[249] *Williamson v. Lee Optical,*[250] *McLaughlin v. Florida,*[251] *United States v. Carolene Products,*[252] *FCC v. Beach Communications,*[253] *Romer v. Evans,*[254] *Cleburne v. Cleburne Living*

---

[248] BVerfGE 90, 145:197 (1994)

[249] *Lindsley v. Natural Carbonic Gas Co.,* 220 U.S. 61 (1910)

[250] *Williamson v. Lee Optical Co.,* 348 U.S. 483 (1955)

[251] *McLaughlin v. Florida,* 379 U.S. 184 (1964)

[252] *United States v. Carolene Products Co.,* 304 U.S. 144 (1938)

[253] *FCC v. Beach Communications, Inc.,* 508 U.S. 307 (1993)

[254] *Romer v. Evans,* 517 U.S. 620 (1996)

Center,[255] *McDonald v. Board of Election Commissioners*,[256] and *New Orleans v. Dukes*.[257]

Thanks to this deferential formula, the drug laws have escaped scrutiny. However, if we look closer, these cases are distinguishable on their facts. To the extent that they were at all dealing with the criminal law none, to my knowledge, were ever imprisoned for failing to abide by their regulations, and as Justice Seiler noted, criticizing the use of *Carolene*,[258] "[t]here is a great difference between a judgment as to whether Congress can declare that a compound of condensed skim milk and coconut oil is 'imitation milk' and a judgment as to whether the legislature can rationally unite marijuana and heroin in a single criminal prohibition."[259] As we have seen, the criminal law is different from all other regulations, for whenever imprisonment is the preferred option the legislature can no longer be afforded unchecked freedom. The legislature has a wide variety of alternatives to choose from other than the criminal law and when such sanctions are applied the burden of evidence belongs to the government.

Courts, however, have failed to recognize this. Even so, to provide an aura of legitimacy to the status quo, they will sometimes speculate as to the "rational" reasons Congress may have had for its decision. In these instances, we are provided with more examples of futile attempts to legitimize the legislature's actions. The courts, for instance, will hypothesize that "the legislative judgment concerning

---

[255] *Cleburne v. Cleburne Living Center, Inc.*, 473 U.S. 432 (1985)

[256] *McDonald v. Board of Election Commissioners*, 394 U.S. 802 (1969)

[257] *New Orleans v. Dukes*, 427 U.S. 297 (1976)

[258] *Carolene Products* upheld the constitutionality of the Filled Milk Act of 1923 and in so doing discredited the judicial interference in the Congressional regulation of interstate commerce to justify deference.

[259] *State v. Mitchell*, 563 S.W.2d 18 (1978) 29 (Seiler J., dissenting)

alcohol and nicotine may well have taken into account . . . the adverse consequences of prohibition, and the economic significance of their production."[260] They will even use reasons of political expediency to explain the legislature's decision,[261] seemingly unaware that a prime basis for the constitutional order is to protect the individual from the undue influence of powerful political factions. And last but not least, they will argue that these drugs are not harmless; that cannabis is more potent today; that politicians may want to criminalize the different drugs in order to fight crime and protect the young; and that legalization would send the wrong message.

But yet again, none of these reasons are sufficient to justify criminalization. What we have been offered as explanations is irrelevant from the perspective of principled law, and the latter examples are not even explanations but merely descriptions of what our officials might have hoped to achieve. As Professor Goldberg points out it is important to separate *descriptions* from *plausible explanations*. Our officials, for example, may say that the drug laws will prevent some degree of possible harm, as they might prevent someone from using a drug and then do something stupid. This, however, is only a description of one of the laws' possible functions and it does not explain why *some* drug users have been chosen to bear the brunt of the legislation. Unfortunately for our officials *this is what is important*. The relevant question at issue in an equal protection analysis is not what

---

[260] *State v. Rao*, 171 Conn. 600 (1976) 606

[261] *People v. Schmidt*, 86 Mich. App. 574 (1978) 581 ("In determining whether the legislative decision to classify and control some substances while not taking a like action as to others was arbitrary, we must also recognize that significant political roadblocks exist which preclude regulating some substances which are known to be dangerous.")

the government sought to achieve, but if it can explain the different punitive treatment of illicit drug users. Unless the state can explain this bit, we are dealing with a constitutional violation, for as Professor Goldstein reminds us: "Where no reasonable explanation exists for the government's singling out of a trait in a given context, what remains 'is a status-based enactment divorced from any factual context from which we could discern a relationship to legitimate state interests—in other words, class legislation."[262]

2.5.4.1. "Half a Loaf"

As we have seen, all the attempts of justifying why alcohol drinkers deserve different treatment from cannabis smokers have failed, but still the argument that "half a loaf is better than one" must be dealt with. For in a last effort to save the status quo, courts will reason that "[w]hile alcoholism constitutes a major social problem, surely it is not valid to justify the adoption of a new abuse on the basis that it is no worse than a presently existing one. The result could only be added social damage from a new source."[263]

The reasoning is flawed for several reasons. First, there is no evidence for concluding that the legal regulation of other drugs than alcohol and tobacco will lead to more social damage. Variables that come into consideration are the following: (1) The assumption that the criminal law has been a successful mechanism in reducing drug use is not borne out by evidence; (2) other factors than criminalization have proven more effective in regulating the use of different drugs;

---

[262] Goldberg, *Equality Without Tiers* (2004) 535 (quoting *Romer*)

[263] *NORML v. Bell*, 488 F.Supp. 123, D.D.C. 1980

and (3) the legal availability of a greater array of drugs is likely to reduce the total of harm to society.[264] The reason is that to the extent other drugs will take the place of alcohol and tobacco, the benefit to society and users will ensure a reduction in total harm. Also, the harms associated with prohibition must be taken into consideration, and when the pros and cons of prohibition are weighted in relation to the pros and cons of legal regulation, the harms associated with prohibition clearly outweigh those associated with regulated supply.

These are all factors that must be taken into consideration and finally, provided that the government's reasons for treating the different classes of drug users differently are not convincing, it is irrelevant if more drug users will become problem drug users. The principle of autonomy carries the greatest weight in any rights analysis and unless the

---

[264] There is evidence to suggest that drug use will not increase, at least by much. A group of experts concluded thus after looking into the subject matter: "Fairly consistently, the finding has been that changes in penalties for use have little effect on rates of use, or on problems arising from effects of the drug. In general, the attempt at deterrence of use or possession though criminal laws have failed." (ROOM ET AL., *CANNABIS POLICY* (2010) 148). This finding has been confirmed by a British Government study called *Drugs, International Comparators*. The report found that tough criminal sentences for drug users makes no difference to the rates of drug use, being that use of illegal substances is influenced by factors "more complex and nuanced than legislation and enforcement alone" and "there is no apparent correlation between the 'toughness' of a country's approach and the prevalence of drug use."

Increase in use, however, is not the only measure of success, as we must factor in that the prohibition regime makes use more dangerous. Scholars have calculated that illegal drug use is between five and ten times more dangerous than legal use. This means that even a highly unlikely five-fold increase in drug use under legalization would not increase the current number of drug deaths. See Ostrowski, *The Moral and Practical Case for Drug Legalization* (1990) 669-70; Duke, *Drug Prohibition: An Unnatural Disaster* (1995) 600 ("even if consumption of legalized drugs increased tenfold under a repeal regime, the physical harms associated with drug use could be less than under prohibition"); and MIKALSEN, *TO END A WAR* (2015) endnotes 45, 71, 77, 79, 82

government can show that its legislation can stand the test of reason, this is a price that we must be prepared to pay.

2.5.4.2. Misapplying Court Doctrine

The bias against illicit drugs is not only evident in the prejudice and different logic that is applied on a case-by-case basis. It is also evident in the way the justices apply their own doctrines to justify their conclusions. We have seen that the *Ravin* court was unique in that it first delineated a general conception of privacy before determining if cannabis use should be included. For this it deserves credit. However, it should be chastised for not following through with proper analysis, as its fundamental rights reasoning was deeply flawed.

One reason why the *Ravin* court set out to formulate a general conception of a right to privacy was that it had to find a definition that included previous cases where the court had found a violation of privacy rights. One important ruling was *Breese v. Smith*, where the Alaska court had held that a school directive that regulated the hear-length of students was an unlawful invasion of privacy. If drug prohibition was to be a lawful infringement of privacy rights, the task was to formulate a general conception that in a meaningful way incorporated the right to choose one's own hair-length while excluding a right to use cannabis.

The court struggled with this task. In the area of privacy analysis the justices found no way of excluding cannabis use, but in the next step of the examination, the fundamental rights analysis, they found a way to disparage the rights claim. In what scholars have argued was a biased and mistaken analysis, the court held the right to choose one's personal hairstyle to be fundamental while it refused to grant the same status to cannabis use. The reasoning behind this decision was that "hairstyle is a highly personal matter involving the individual and his body," while cannabis use was not. To justify this position, the court simply took for granted that "few would believe they have been deprived of something of critical importance if deprived of marijuana, though they would be if stripped of control over their personal appearances."[265]

It is for good reason that scholars have criticized the *Ravin* court for this analysis. As Professor Husak has pointed out:

"This basis for contrasting the degree of protection offered to hair length in *Breese* from that offered to marijuana use in *Ravin* is deficient. First, no empirical data are cited to support the court's conjecture about what 'few would believe.' Persons who smoke marijuana might feel just as strongly as about their preference as persons who violate the school ordinance governing hair length. Moreover, it is unclear that the degree of protection offered by the right of privacy should depend on the numbers of persons who have or lack the relevant beliefs. Third, and most significant, the question is rigged to enable the court to justify its answer. I concede that more persons would be outraged if 'stripped of control over their personal appearance' than if 'deprived of marijuana.' But the terms of the comparison are flawed and misleading. The first part of the comparison is very general and the second is very specific. Imagine how the

---

[265] *Ravin v. State*, 537 P.2d at 502

question would have been answered if the first part of the comparison were very specific and the second were very general. How would persons feel if 'stripped of control over what they are allowed to put into their bodies' relative to a 'deprivation of shoulder-length hair'? Clearly, the outcome of such a determination would be very different. To be meaningful and unbiased, the examples to be compared must invoke the same level of generality. On that basis it is hard to decide whether persons care more over what they are permitted to put into their bodies than about control over their personal appearance. I see no reason to regard either matter as more important, basic, or fundamental than the other."[266]

2.5.5. Emptying Words of Meaning

Having reviewed the many ways by which the courts will deny drug users an effective remedy, we have seen (1) that unprincipled, ad hoc reasoning is offered as an excuse to defer to the legislature and (2) that none of the attempts to justify the status quo are valid from a perspective of principled law. Even so, as long as the courts can hypothesize some reason for the legislature's actions, that is all it takes to close their eyes to the injustice that is our drug laws. In the end, therefore, we find that the root of all this evil is the courts' idea of "rationality" and "arbitrariness," which is so disconnected from reality that it adds insult to injury.

---

[266] Husak, *Two Rationales for Drug Policy*, in FISH (ED.), *HOW TO LEGALIZE DRUGS* (1998) 44-45

2.5.5.1. Problems With "Rational Basis"

We have seen that the enforcement of drug prohibition is highly contested and many scholars[267] and reports[268] conclude that the drug law has failed to protect the welfare of society. According to these sources, prohibition has done the opposite. They affirm that its impact on the supply and demand of illicit drugs has not only been negligible, but that it has generated death, disease, and criminal activity at the individual level while destroying communities and wholesome values at the collective level. To the most perceptive, this was clear 50 years ago,[269] and the evidence today is overwhelming.[270]

This being so, it should be evident that the courts' rational basis test is worthless. The prohibitionists' presumptions have all been refuted, and yet courts will hold that the drug

---

[267] The list of professionals is too long, as it includes just about everyone who knows a thing or two about drug policy. However, as examples of collective efforts, a group of 500 luminaries from around the world—including Nobel Laureate Milton Friedman, former Secretary of State George Shultz, and former UN Secretary General Javier Perez de Cueller—have signed an open letter the U.S. President and Congress arguing that the global War on Drugs is causing more harm than good and urging that alternatives be considered. Another group of 770 academics wrote to the UN Secretary General in 1998, declaring that "the global War on Drugs is now causing more harm than drug abuse itself," and asking the bureaucrats "to initiate a truly open and honest dialogue regarding the future of global drug control policies; one in which fear, prejudice and punitive prohibitions yield to common sense, science, public health and human rights." (see http://www.drugpolicy.org/ publications-resources/sign-letters/public-letter-kofi-annan/ungass-public-letter-kofi-annan-signato)

[268] See list in MIKALSEN, *TO END A WAR* (2015) 162-63 (n.73)

[269] See e.g., KAPLAN, *MARIJUANA: THE NEW PROHIBITION* (1971); Kadish, *The Crisis of Overcriminalization* (1968)

[270] MIKALSEN, *TO END A WAR* (2015) at 161-63 (n.72-73) & at 165-77 (n.77-85). See also BERTRAM ET AL., *DRUG WAR POLITICS* (1996) 33-54; BECKER, *TO END THE WAR ON DRUGS* (2014); ALEXANDER, *THE NEW JIM CROW* (2011); ESCOHOTADO, *A BRIEF HISTORY OF DRUGS* (1999); DUKE & CROSS, *AMERICA'S LONGEST WAR* (1993) 78-200; WISOTSKY, *BEYOND THE WAR ON DRUGS* (1990); MILLER, *THE CASE FOR LEGALIZING DRUGS* (1991)

law meets the rationality criteria. How can this be? Is it not self-evident that "rationally related" must mean something more than a rational relationship between our leaders' assumptions and their actions? No matter what kind of mad hatters we put in charge, this will always be the case. In the 1600s, the burning of witches was rationally related to the goal of ridding the world of evil; in the 1940s, the Nazis' eradication efforts were rationally related to the belief in the superiority of the Aryan race; and in our day, the drug laws are rationally related to the belief that drug users must be persecuted. No matter the time and place, our leaders' actions will reflect their beliefs—and all these beliefs will be "rational" to the people who hold them. But what kind of justice system will be content with this standard? It has proven utterly useless in preventing the abuse of power, and doesn't this fact—that it is worthless as a standard for protecting human rights—merit consideration?

To put it another way, does not "rationally related," by necessity, imply a certain quality of belief? Does not "rationally related" imply that a law must be *functionally* related to the goal it seeks to obtain? That it must be *morally* related to values that are said to guide us? That it must be *meaningfully* related to the ideals and principles of social contract thinking?

Few would object to this. And so should not "rationally related", by necessity, imply an opportunity to assess whether in fact our leaders' beliefs are rationally grounded in the first place? What use is this term if it ignores (or rejects as irrelevant) whether policies are enacted on false presumptions? The fact that "rationally related" must imply a certain validity of belief is everywhere insinuated and articulated in American law,[271] and yet we find ourselves in a situation where the drug laws fail this standard—and where the courts for more than fifty years have denied the opportunity to prove this point.

2.5.5.2. The Courts' Definition of "Arbitrary"

The courts' idea of "rationally related" is intimately connected with their use of "arbitrary," and the problem with the former is brought to light by the latter.

In effect, the courts will hold that if they can imagine some reason for justifying a prohibition it is not arbitrary. Never mind if the reasons they imagine are wrong; never mind if the envisioned connection between means and ends is not there; never mind if the facts and the consequences of the law undermine any asserted reason for enacting the law. None of this matter: If they can imagine a rationalization, the law fulfills the criteria to be justified under the rational basis test.

To more serious-minded individuals this selective notion of "rationality" and "arbitrariness" is another example of the intellectual despondency that has eaten its way into the heart of American law. It should be a source of worry and contemplation as this is Orwellian Newspeak. The justices

---

[271] *People v. Braun*, 330 N.Y.S.2d 397, 941, 69 Misc. 2d 682 (1972) ("To sustain legislation under the 'police power,' the operation of the law must in some degree tend to prevent offense or evil or preserve public health, morals, or welfare; it should appear that the means used are reasonably necessary for accomplishment of the purpose and not unduly oppressive upon individuals."); Jackson, *Putting Rationality Back Into the Rational Basis Test* (2011) 543 ("Where the legislative enactment infringes on an identified liberty interest, it is not enough that some legislator might have thought that there was a rational relationship. Liberty demands an actual rational link between the means and the ends.")

are effectively saying that "in this day and age words have no meaning other than that which we put into them. If we like it, then it is 'rational' and if we do not it is irrational and arbitrary—but do not expect us to justify our claims with empiricism. We have no use for reality, we make our own."

This is the outlandish notion that American citizens are expected to endure; this is the contemptible state of affairs that is American law. On this basis 1.5 million people are every year deprived of their freedom; and on this basis 40 million Americans are supposed to live as criminals—all in order to sustain conceited egos and a government that has long since abandoned the rule of law.

These are harsh words, but not unfounded. Everybody knows that "reasonable" and "arbitrary" must refer to some objectively verifiable state of facts. Under the Canadian system, for instance, a law is arbitrary whenever it fails to conform to the criteria set out by the proportionality analysis—that is, whenever it fails to reflect a correct balancing of the individual's right to liberty and society's need for protection.[272] Several justices at the Canadian Supreme Court have held the drug law to be an arbitrary— and therefore unlawful—infringement on these terms,[273] and we find the same definition in international human rights law. At the European Court of Human Rights and in the United Nations system, the terms "unlawful" and "arbitrary" are interchangeable, and as the UN Human Rights Committee stated:

---

[272] *Carter v. Canada* (Attorney General), 2015 SCC 5, [2015] 1 S.C.R. 331, at para. 83.

[273] *R. v. Malmo-Levine*; *R. v. Caine* 2003 SCC 74, 582, 729 (LeBel & Deschamps dissenting)

"In the Committee's view the expression 'arbitrary interference' can also extend to interference provided for under the law. *The introduction of the concept of arbitrariness is intended to guarantee that even interference provided for by law should be in accordance with the provisions, aims and objectives of the Covenant [i.e., first principles] and should be, in any event, reasonable in the particular circumstances.*"[274]

None of this is controversial. It is the same definition that scholars and judges all over the world, including some in the United States,[275] abide by, and that a majority of American justices reject this definition can only be taken as a testimony to the fact that the system of law has hit rock bottom. After all, what better indication can we find that the U.S. system has left behind all pretense of respectability? To anyone who cares about words and meaning this is, to say the least, an embarrassing state of affairs. Nonetheless, this is the only way that US justices can bridge the gap between theory and

---

[274] Ibid. (emphasis mine)

[275] Justice Adkins of the Florida Supreme Court objected to the current state of affairs when he said that "[t]here must be more than a hypothetical rational basis for a classification"; that in the real world "valid and substantial reason for classifications" had to be given; and that this required "a just, fair and practical basis" for the classification—one "based on a real difference which is reasonably related to the subject and purpose of the regulation." He continued to say that "to determine the rationality of a law the Court must look at the purpose the law serves, the facts involved, the impact of the law upon citizens and the relationship between the law and these factors." He made it clear that this was not the case when considering the classification of marijuana and that, therefore, "the statute should be held unconstitutional and the judgment of the trial court reversed." *Hamilton v. State*, 366 So. 2d 8 (1978) 12 (Adkins J., dissenting). See also Fiss, *Groups and the Equal Protection Clause* (1976) 111 ("In most cases it is not a question of whether the criterion and end are related or unrelated, but a question of how well they are related. A criterion may be deemed arbitrary even if it is related to the purpose, but only poorly so.")

practice, and so this is the way it must be until Americans once again take matters of law and government seriously.

3

HAWAII: A MICROCOSM OF THE MACROCOSM

"It has not been shown that consumption of marijuana is any more harmful than a comparable consumption of alcohol and it is doubtful that the presently known effects of marijuana are as adverse as those of alcohol. Until legitimate research indicates otherwise, the harm created by placing a criminal sanction on the activity of a significant percentage of our population who would otherwise be law abiding citizens far outweighs any present benefit to be derived from the effects of classifying marijuana as a narcotic. There is no logical or otherwise rational reason for our society, on the basis of a law that has little or no merit in its application, to continue to make criminals out of and consequently alienate the youth of today." [276]

—Justice Kobayashi—

NOW THAT WE HAVE reviewed the bigger picture and how the dynamic between principled and unprincipled reasoning plays out in the discourse on drug policy, we shall end this case study by focusing on Hawaii. In the history of constitutional challenges this state is unique. Nowhere did

---

[276] *State v. Kantner*, 493 P.2d 306 (1972) at 320 (Kobayashi, J., dissenting)

principled reasoning come closer to carrying the day in court and nowhere is the dynamic between principled and unprincipled reasoning better exposed. In the following therefore, I will rely on the second Justice Levinson's *Mallan* dissent, a noble work which presents the battle between these two types of reasoning as it played out at the Hawai'i Supreme Court between 1972 and 1998.[277]

3.1. The Kantner Court

The story begins with a confusing victory to the proponents of arbitrary reasoning in *State v. Kantner*,[278] where they won the day even though a majority concluded that marijuana use was a fundamental right. In this stunning piece of constitutional history, principled reasoning would have proved victorious if not for the event that one of its advocates, Justice Abe, felt compelled to affirm the judgment of the trial court. He, himself, was personally opposed to the result, but because appellants from the outset had accepted the prohibition of marijuana as a reasonable and legitimate exercise of the police power (they only contended that the inclusion of marijuana in the narcotic drug statute was unreasonable and violated the Due Process Clauses of the federal and state Constitution) he found it unreasonable to hold that the state should have met its burden of proof on this point.

Levinson and Kobayashi, the other principled reasoners, disagreed, believing it to be sufficiently clear that the merits

---

[277] *State v. Mallan*, 86 Haw. 440, 950 P.2d 178 (1998) 193-248 (Levinson J., dissenting)

[278] *Kantner*, 53 Haw. 327, 493 P.2d 306 (1972)

of the case dictated that the laws prohibiting the possession of marijuana be held unconstitutional. However, because of the failure of the appellants to frame the issue correctly, the extraordinary fact that most of the justices agreed that the prohibition of marijuana possession was unconstitutional did not have much impact.

It is ironic that the only time in the history of drug law challenges when a majority were principled reasoners, the appellants underestimated the unconstitutional nature of the law and the willingness of the justices to deal with it. Be that as it may, the legacy of *Kantner* was three carefully crafted dissenting opinions—opinions that to this day remain among the top five examples of FC reasoning delivered by any American court.

Unfortunately, this was the only time in constitutional history that the stars were sufficiently aligned for principled reasoning to have had an impact on the evolution of drug policy. The year after, in 1973, Justice Abe retired, and Justice Levinson retired in 1974.

3.2. The Baker Court

So it came to pass that in 1975, when the next challenge reached the Supreme Court with *State v. Baker,*[279] it was an open question if the new court would honor the analysis put forth in *Kantner*. As it was the only outcome-dispositive and controlling authority on the subject in the jurisdiction, the appellants had every reason to believe that they would—and things started out on a positive vibe. Encouraged by the

---

[279] 56 Haw. 271, 535 P.2d 1394 (1975)

reasoning of the *Kantner* trio, the district court placed on the state the burden of showing clearly and convincingly that prohibiting the possession of marijuana was a proper exercise of the police power. After carefully reviewing the factual picture, the court held that the state had not met this burden and that the law violated the due process clauses of the state and federal Constitution. The prosecution appealed the decision, and the time came for the new court to show its true colors.

On appeal, the primary question for the majority was if the trial court had been wrong in placing the burden of evidence on the state. Unsurprisingly (if one considers the prevalence of arbitrary law) they held that it had, and their opinion proved to be the traditional display of surrealistic reasoning that inevitably follows from false doctrines. According to the majority, the district court, in beginning with a presumption of liberty, had "approach[ed] the issue . . . with the wrong end of the stick."[280] The right end of the stick, according to the court, would have been to ask whether there was a fundamental right to smoke marijuana and from there on get in the line with the previous decisions which held that no such right existed.

As the problems with this reasoning are spelled out elsewhere, I shall not elaborate on this bit. However, to arrive at this conclusion, the *Baker* court had to perform quite a miscarriage of justice. The quandary for the *Baker* court was that there was a strong precedent in Hawai'i jurisprudence for sustaining the *Kantner* trio's analysis. In a series of cases[281]

---

[280] Id. at 276-82, 535 P.2d at 1398

[281] *Territory v. Kraft*, 33 Haw. 397 (1935); *State v. Lee*, 51 Haw.516, 517, 465 P.2d 573, 575 (1970); *State v. Shigematsu*, 52 Haw.604, 607, 483 P.2d 997, 999 (1971); *State v. Cotton*, 55 Haw.138, 516 P.2d 709 (1973)

the court had already defined principled limits on the police power, and according to this analysis the state had the burden of proof. To shoulder its burden, it had to (1) show that the interests of the public required such interference, and (2) that the means were reasonably necessary for the accomplishment of the purpose and not unduly oppressive upon individuals.

Taking its own doctrines seriously, then, the court would have had to invalidate the drug law as being an unconstitutional exercise of the police power. The *Baker* court, however, would not be discouraged, and with the injudicious logic that always accompanies such decisions the majority went on a rampage to destroy whatever authority FC reasoning had had. As Justice Levinson himself said on the matter, "the majority opinion . . . effected a deconstruction and reconstruction of this court's jurisprudential 'past' that is utterly Orwellian in its scope and methodology. Indeed, the Baker majority literally 'went by the book.'"[282]

In his dissent Levinson documents how the majority rewrote the past by ignoring reality and reason, but as we have discussed the various ways by which the courts will disparage constitutionally valid rights-claims, the *Baker* court's odyssey into the night shall not be rehearsed. Suffice to say that it followed the tired old recipe. And as Levinson noted, so it was that "the *Baker* majority managed to ignore the unignorable: that a mere three years previously, a . . . majority of the *Kantner* court . . . had agreed that, as a matter of constitutional law, the police power of the state did not extend to the criminalization of mere possession of marijuana for personal use."[283]

---

[282] *Mallan*, 86 Haw. 440, 950 P.2d 178 (1998) 216 (Levinson J., dissenting)

[283] Id.216 (Levinson J., dissenting)

However, there was still one capable FC reasoner left on the court. This was Justice Kobayashi. A former Attorney General, he stood his ground, reviewed the factual picture, and in a lone dissent was "compelled to conclude that the statute in question constitutes an arbitrary and capricious exercise of police powers by the [state]."[284] As he said:

> "In my opinion . . . the real purpose of the criminalization of possession of marijuana is simply to perpetuate society's prejudice against marijuana; a prejudice which I believe is based mainly upon inaccurate information. Clearly, the only confirmed harm of marijuana is not in marijuana per se, but the laws which criminalize the possessor. The lives and careers of many thousands of possessors have been damaged or destroyed irrationally and oppressively. The interest of society generally has been seriously harmed by the unnecessary criminalization of a large segment of the people. Organized crime or crimes have been fostered by the act of the [state] in proscribing the possession of marijuana. In the exercise of [the state's] police powers, the law is clear: To justify the state in interposing its authority on behalf of the public, it must appear, first, that the interests of the public require such interference; and, second, that the means are reasonably necessary for the accomplishment of the purpose, and not unduly oppressive upon individuals.
>
> . . . In my opinion, the statute prohibiting the possession of marijuana fails to meet the above test. Mere debatable possible harm of marijuana on the individual user does not justify the [state] in interposing its authority on behalf of the public. Assuming *arguendo* [that] justification exists in proscribing the possession of marijuana, the

---

[284] Id.218 (Levinson J., dissenting)

means used to discourage the individual possession of marijuana is not reasonably necessary. The means used has not only failed to accomplish the purpose, but is irrational and unduly oppressive upon the individual marijuana users. . . . I would affirm the result of the trial court's judgment for the reasons stated."[285]

3.3. The Renfro Court

Six months after *Baker,* with *State v. Renfro,* another constitutional challenge came before the Supreme Court.[286] The appellants, however, stood no chance. Having already rewritten the past into a picture more to its liking, the majority simply referred to *Baker* and left the appellants with the impossible task of convincing a panel of indisposed justices that there were meaningful limits to the police power. In the mind of the majority, this was hardly the case and the appellants lost. As Justice Levinson summarized the proceedings:

"What is particularly striking about the majority opinion in *Renfro* is its mantraesque, rote quality. Although the constitutional constraints established in *Kraft* and *Lee* on the state's police power were acknowledged in theory, they seem essentially to have atrophied to a null set. Indeed, the *Renfro* majority opinion virtually turns the Kraft/Lee analysis on its head. Gone was the proposition, from which 'we start,' 'that where an individual's

---

[285] Baker, 56 Haw. at 285, 288-92, 535 P.2d at 1402, 1404-06 (Kobayashi, J., concurring and dissenting) (some brackets and ellipsis points in original and some added) (footnotes omitted)

[286] *State v. Renfro,* 56 Haw. 501, 542 P.2d 366 (1975)

conduct, or class of individuals' conduct, does not directly harm others, the public interest is not affected and is not properly the subject of the police power of the legislature.' And in the face of a legislative determination 'that the conduct of a particular class of people recklessly affects their physical well-being and that the consequent physical injury and death is so widespread as to be of grave concern to the public,' not only was it no longer required, as a precondition of the state's exercise of the police power, that 'the incidence and severity of the physical harm be statistically demonstrated to the satisfaction of the court,' but the diametric opposite seemed to have become the case: if the incidence and severity of the physical harm was 'inconclusive,' and the state of 'scientific knowledge' was 'incomplete,' then the legislature could exercise the police power in whatever way it wanted.

In short, the *Renfro* majority seemed to have completely forgotten the 'direct harm to others/ statistically demonstrated secondary social harm' circumscription of the constitutional exercise the state's police power so carefully explicated in *Kraft* and *Lee*. That being so, it is little wonder that the *Renfro* majority regarded the constitutional right of privacy—if it really believed there was one at all, having never found an instance in which it took precedence over anything else— as being of such minor, non-fundamental importance that individual privacy was invariably obliged to 'give way' to legislative whim and speculation."[287]

---

[287] *Mallan*, 86 Haw. 440, 950 P.2d 178 (1998) 221-22 (Levinson J., dissenting) (citations omitted)

Justice Kobayashi, having stated his position with sufficient lucidity in *Kantner* and *Baker*, wrote a one-sentence dissent, holding that he disagreed for the reasons stated in *Baker*.[288] Significantly, however, his opinion in that case had apparently persuaded Judge Sodetani, who joined in the *Renfro* dissent. Accordingly, as in *Kantner*, the marijuana law was found constitutional by a single vote.

Then, on December 29, 1978, Justice Kobayashi retired from the court. For some time there were no more justices capable of principled opposition to the impiety which had eaten its way into the heart of the American legal system. From then on a presumption of constitutionality ruled supreme and the police power was, as far as drug policy goes, boundless. It was under these conditions that a unanimous Hawai'i Supreme Court, on May 21, 1979, handed down a per curiam opinion in *State v. Bachman*.[289] The court simply stated that it found Bachman's contention to be without merit and referred to what it had said in *Baker* and *Renfro*.

3.4. The Mallan Court

It would be 20 years before another justice capable of FC reasoning emerged to challenge the status quo. That honor went to the second Justice Levinson who took on the majority in *Mallan*.

What made this case so interesting was that by the time *Mallan* was decided a right to privacy had been added to the Hawai'i Constitution. In 1978 a Constitutional Convention

---

[288] *Renfro*, 56 Haw. at 507, 542 P.2d at 370 (Kobayashi, J., dissenting)

[289] 61 Haw. 71, 595 P.2d 287 (1979)

had gathered to provide better constitutional protection against arbitrary infringements on autonomy/liberty rights. As a result, Article I of the State Constitution was amended by adding a new section which read: "The right of the people to privacy is recognized and shall not be infringed without the showing of a compelling state interest. The legislature shall take affirmative steps to implement this right."

The question now was how to interpret this amendment. Could it be, as the proponents of the drug law predictably would argue, that it only referred to a small group of privacy rights, such as those already given preferred protection by the courts? Or could it be that it referred to privacy rights in general—that is, that it protected *any and all* autonomy and liberty rights from undue interference?

Looking at the reports of the Committee that prepared this new amendment, there was no doubt that it meant exactly what it said. The Standing Committee spoke of a "right to personal autonomy," "to be let alone," and continued:

> "It should be emphasized that this right is not an absolute one, but, because similar to the right of free speech, it is so important in value that it can be infringed upon only by the showing of a compelling state interest. If the State is able to show a compelling state interest, the right of the group will prevail over the privacy rights or the right of the individual. However, in view of the important nature of this right, the State must use the least restrictive means should it desire to interfere with the right. Your Committee expects that at times the interests of national security, law enforcement, the interest of the State to protect the lives of citizens or other similar interests will be strong enough to override the right to privacy. *It is not the intent of your Committee to grant a license to*

individuals to violate the right of others, but rather to grant the individual full control over his life, absent the showing of a compelling state interest to protect his security and that of others."[290]

The Constitutional Convention endorsed the report in its entirety, and so there could be no doubt about the legislature's intent: It was to protect the individual's right to be let alone and to have *"full control over his life" in the absence of a "compelling state interest."* In other words, strict scrutiny would apply, and the government would have to demonstrate that its action had been structured with precision; that it was narrowly tailored to serve legitimate objectives; and that it had selected the least drastic means for achieving its objectives.

Not only that, but the Standing Committee stated that "the importance of this amendment is that it establishes that certain rights deserve special judicial protection from majority rule. It recognizes that there will always be a dynamic tension between majority rule, which is the basis of a democratic society, and the rights of individuals to do as they choose, which is the basis of freedom, and your Committee believes that this amendment recognizes the high value that individuality has in society. Your Committee, by equating privacy with the first amendment rights, intends that the right be considered a fundamental right and that interference with the activities protected by it be minimal."[291]

As we can see, the legislature most definitely put another act of principled reasoning/legislation on the books and the

---

[290] *Mallan*, 86 Haw. 440, 950 P.2d 178 (1998) 225 (Levinson J., dissenting) (emphasis mine)

[291] Id.

Supreme Court unanimously recognized all of this in *State v. Kam*,[292] where it held the prohibition of obscene materials in the home unconstitutional.

This being so, the stage was perfectly set for another constitutional challenge to the drug law. Things were looking good for the appellant, Lloyd Mallan, as the court needed only apply its own doctrine with some consistency—then the presumption of liberty would be honored and the state would have to provide a compelling justification for interfering with his rights. The majority, however, would have none of it. Except for Levinson's powerful dissent, the justices would not include drug use as a protected privacy right and yet again arbitrary law carried the day.

Considering that the legislature so clearly had put an act of principled reasoning on the books, how was this possible?

Again, the answer is found in human psychology, where the FC/NC model puts autonomy-oriented and tyranny-oriented individuals at different end. And presuming that more sinister reasons were not involved, the answer is that the minds of NC individuals operate in a closed-loop system whereby the implications of FC reasoning will consistently be ignored. They will ignore the implications of higher-order reasoning because they are not yet ready to expand their horizons—and they are not ready to expand their horizons because it entails an expansion of Self that can be frightening to the ego. Our identity is closely associated with the beliefs we hold and it takes a certain amount of maturity to leave old belief-structures behind. To do so is to leave the old idea of Self behind, and this can only be done when the ego is not too entranced by fear. Fear is the one thing that prevents people

---

[292] *State v. Kam*, 69 Haw. 483, 748 P.2d 372 (1988)

from moving forward, as each step is a like a small death to the ego.

It is this "petite-mort" that ensures that so many humans will resist change—and this fear of ego-death is why so many prefer insanity to reason. Following reason, after all, entails a willingness to leave old ideas behind and this is impossible if our identity is too attached to old belief-structures. The further towards the NC-end we operate, the more fervently we will cling on to the old sense of self, and so those at this level will reject reason to escape whatever conclusions they would have to embrace by stepping into a greater, more coherent frame of reference.

The *Mallan* majority was no different. These justices showed no willingness to check the validity of their presumptions, and because the enemy image was beyond reproach the justices could not accept the implications of the legislature's principled position. Something—but not the drug law—had to yield, and we shall see how they solved the problem.

3.4.1. The Mallan Court's Defective Privacy Analysis

For an unbiased observer, the *Mallan* court had a huge problem if it were to side with the drug law. To begin with, the Hawai'i Constitution had its own privacy clause, and it left state courts "free to give broader privacy protection than that given by the federal constitution."[293] Now, as we have seen, the premise that privacy rights are better protected by

---

[293] *Kam*, 69 Haw. at 491, 748 P.2d at 377

constitutions with an explicit privacy protection clause is itself flawed. It is the underlying principles that determine where the line that separates the individual from the collective's sphere shall be drawn and if the Constitution has an enumerated privacy clause is irrelevant. Be that as it may, the *Mallan* majority recognized that "our case law and the text of our constitution appear to invite this court to look beyond the federal standards in interpreting the right to privacy,"[294] and the justices went on to the next question, whether there was a constitutionally protected right to possess marijuana for personal use.

In pondering this, the justices looked to the legislature process. It is a long-recognized principle of law that the Constitution must be interpreted with due regard to the intent of the framers and the people adopting it and that the fundamental principle in interpreting a constitutional provision is to give effect to that intent. Hence, the task at hand was to look at the committee reports and debates in the Constitutional Convention where the privacy clause was adopted.

Looking at this, it was clear that the legislature had done its job properly. It was clear that the committee members followed in the founders' footsteps and that their intention was to provide enhanced security against undue government interference. This could only be done by emphasizing the importance of respecting the underlying principles of the constitutional order, and so the committee members sought to set principled limits that protected the privacy of individuals. This was the whole point of the legislature's work—*this was the intention*. However, even though the legislature had made

---

[294] *Mallan*, 86 Haw. 440, 950 P.2d 178 (1998) 186

its intentions clear, this did not hinder the majority from refusing to act. Never mind that the right to privacy was *a general* right. Never mind that it only excluded those activities which the government had good reasons for criminalizing. And never mind that the statute explicitly said that *the only* way to determine if this was the case was by the state showing that it had a compelling interest in prohibiting the activity in question.

We have already seen how the impact of an enemy image (and the psychological incentives behind it) will incapacitate those in its grip. Its power takes precedence before all else, and so it is that, to comply with the demands of the enemy image, logic will be turned on its head.[295] We have seen how this results in different standards of harm, culpability, dignity, decency, as well as other mindless ramblings, and the *Mallan* majority was no different. Even though the legislature had stated that the purpose of the privacy clause was "to grant the individual full control over his life, absent the showing of a compelling state interest," it proved impossible for these justices to cope with the implications. Surely this could not include drug use? Surely it could not mean that the state had

---

[295] An interesting example of the self-refuting and paradoxical reasoning that results is found in Tribe and Dorf's essay on levels of generality in the definition of rights. In this article they demonstrate the folly of Justice Scalia's attempt to define rights at the most specific level. However, after first noting the importance of "seek[ing] unifying principles that will push constitutional law toward rationality," and stating that "rationality dictates that one does not segregate the reasoning applicable to one medium from the reasoning that has prevailed with respect to other media," they suddenly, when speaking of drug policy, forget to apply their own rules of construction. Instead, they fall into the same trap as Scalia, claiming that "just as the Constitution's repeated references to private property render fatuous any asserted right to steal, so the concern for the preservation of human life expressed in both the Fifth and Fourteenth Amendments undercuts a fundamental liberty interest in assisting an otherwise healthy individual to poison herself." Tribe & Dorf, *Levels of Generality in the Definition of Rights* (1990) 1070, 1071, 1107

to show good reasons for denying people this right? Surely the drug law should not have to be defended?

For some reason, the idea of an effective remedy was repugnant to the majority and they had to ensure that the legislature's exact words and intention was rendered null and void. This was done by resorting to the traditional way of disparaging rights-claims, the fundamental rights analysis. They began by stating that "[t]here is no question that the right of privacy embodied in article I, section 6 is a fundamental right in and of itself. Any infringement of the right to privacy must be subjected to the compelling state interest test. Thus, the only analysis this court need utilize when testing a right to privacy claim such as Mallan's is whether the conduct prohibited by law is entitled to protection under article I, section 6."[296]

When it came to this the answer was easy. The justices did not have to look to any other authority than their own biased notions to find that marijuana use could not possibly be protected by the privacy clause, for even if the legislature had opted for across-the-board protection the court could not imagine that the delegates adopting the privacy provision could foresee the implications of their actions. The justices felt sure that if the committee members' personal preferences (read: prejudices) were allowed to count, they would not have meant what they said. It was simply unthinkable that the legislature would have encouraged a principled application of the law if it meant that the drug laws could be subjected to meaningful scrutiny. And so, interpreting the privacy provision according to their own subjective preferences, the *Mallan* majority held that "[i]f the delegates had intended

---

[296] *Mallan*, 86 Haw. 440, 950 P.2d 178 (1998) 247 (JJ., Klein and Nakayama concurring)

such a result, surely they would have placed an explicit reference in the committee reports. Instead, the committee reports contain no mention of the legalization of illicit drugs."[297]

Such an interpretation is what we can expect from those operating at the NC level. Never mind that this interpretation would undermine the purpose of the constitutional order. Never mind that according to this interpretation the Privacy Clause would be useless, its words void of any objective meaning. Never mind that to arrive at this conclusion they had to rely on the self-refuting logic and incoherent reasoning we have previously discussed. This is a price NC individuals are willing to pay to keep their biased notions intact.

If it were not for the psychological incentives behind the enemy image, however, the justices would have come to grips with the duplicity inherent in such reasoning. They would have understood that it was the mindset of immature individuals at work; individuals who insist on holding two contradictory ideas at the same time, who would like to keep both, and who therefore refused to reconsider the implications of their position. A healthy mind—a mind ready to evolve—could not possibly live with this dissonance. An individual at this level of growth would have understood that a dissonance between two simultaneously held beliefs were an indication of mental sickness. She would have understood that two conflicting ideas could not both be true, that one would have to yield, and that the moral compass of this predicament was found in accepting the implications of principled reasoning. Consequently, she would be open to the light of reason, follow it to its conclusion and discard the

---

[297] Id. 186

incompatible idea. In doing so she would not be worse off. Instead, she would have arrived at a higher, more evolved and coherent level of reality, one where her sense of self was not entwined with disserving notions and falsely held convictions.

For the *Mallan* majority, however, this was not an option. Relying on the fundamental rights doctrine, they took the coward's way out and opted for the rational basis test. Consequently, it was yet again for the defendant to prove that "the government's action was clearly arbitrary and unreasonable, having no substantial relation to the public health, safety, morals, or general welfare" to a court that already had made up its mind. According to the majority, the idea of using a more demanding test, such as the one advanced by the dissent, was rejected as outmoded and discredited thinking. It belonged to an era of constitutional history from which the court had long departed, and the court had no intention of returning to an age when the presumption of liberty held sway. According to the majority, that would "lead to dangerous and unprecedented results," and "the dissent's general methodology present[ed] a significant danger."[298]

3.4.2. The Majority's Fear of Principled Reasoning

To higher evolved individuals it is difficult to imagine the "danger" in abiding by the doctrines of reason. To them, it is impossible to see how a state having to justify its criminal laws would be a threat to anything other than arbitrary and

---

[298] Id. 192

unjust laws and the advocates of tyrannical government. But again, NC individuals feel very much threatened by this. The majority admitted as much. To them, the problem with Levinson's reasoning was that it "decriminalizes the use and possession of virtually all contraband drugs used within the home or wherever a person believes he is 'in privacy.'"[299] As Justice Levinson replied in his dissent, this may or may not be the case, depending on whether or not such a result is the outcome of a properly applied balancing test.

Levinson's response, however, is not persuasive to proponents of arbitrary law. Being blinded by an exaggerated enemy image, they will resist any urge to follow the implications of principled reasoning. Under no conditions will they double-check the validity of this enemy image, and as the light of reason cannot guide them, they will (1) overcomplicate or (2) oversimplify the issue. In either case their analysis will be off, and they imagine that if principled reasoning proved triumphant, all restrictions on drugs would have to be abandoned and hell would break loose.

This is not the case. First of all, we are not talking about an either-or, where we must choose between two extremes. If the prohibition of cannabis should fail to pass constitutional muster it might be that some regulation is still feasible; its sales might be taxed and controlled, its use might be prohibited in public places, and so on. Secondly, even if cannabis prohibition should violate liberty/autonomy rights, it might be that the prohibition of other drugs is constitutional; it all depends on the factual picture and if the state can demonstrate with sufficient evidence that its premises for advocating a prohibition are sound. If the

---

[299] Id. 189

government's argument is sound, prohibition will have no problem with first principles and the law will have proven its validity. But if there is a problem, it will be because the drug law does not serve its stated purpose and because it fails to balance the rights of the individual against the needs of society. *In either case* the best argument wins and the public good will be served—and so, whatever the result, there is *absolutely no need* to fear the outcome.

Prohibitionists' fear of principled reasoning, therefore, is not rational. The majority's warning that it would lead to "dangerous and unprecedented results" is simply a testimony to the power of the enemy images, as we are dealing with emotional resistance. As long as people remain spellbound by the enemy image of drugs no reasoning, no matter how coherent, will make a difference and any objective inquiry will be shunned. History, as well as the replies to principled reasoning are evidence of this. As we have seen, all the objections raised are proven irrelevant, and while the *Mallan* majority rehearsed a few of these already refuted objections, they also added another. Explaining why Levinson's reasoning was so "dangerous," the majority not only claimed that its "expansive interpretation circumvents the natural development of the right to privacy in two respects: (1) it removes from the developmental process the voice of the people as expressed by legislative action, and (2) it eschews careful case-by-case development of the right to privacy by the courts."[300]

With respect to the first point, this is of no concern. After all, we are not merely a democracy; we are a democracy governed by the rule of law, and the rule of law dictates that

---

[300] Id.189

the individual has rights that supersede the rule of ignorant and prejudiced beliefs, no matter how commonly or deeply held. As the Hawai'i legislature had reminded the court, "there will always be a dynamic tension between majority rule, which is the basis of a democratic society, and the rights of individuals to do as they choose, which is the basis of freedom," and the right to privacy is one of those fundamental rights that "deserve special judicial protection from majority rule."[301] Hence, what the majority of the voters want does not necessarily matter, and this objection is another of those kneejerk responses that most judges will use to hide from constitutional responsibilities.[302]

With respect to the second point, this is equally irrelevant. After all, there is nothing in the doctrines of law that speak against a full change of direction whenever rights-violations are discovered. To the contrary, it would be a gross miscarriage of justice to disregard evidence of failure only to retreat from the status quo in incremental steps. The only reason why such an advance would appeal to some is that it would lessen the embarrassment felt by the purveyors and defenders of the drug laws. It is, no doubt, difficult for this lot to face the facts and to confront the reality of their actions. Quite a few would become rabid at the notion of immediate repeal, and so, to sustain their delusive pretenses of virtue, one could argue that we need another 50 years to do away with the drug laws completely.

---

[301] Id. 225

[302] "The judiciary is obligated to examine the reasonableness of legislative classifications and to declare them unconstitutional when it finds them to be so. In the words of Chief Justice Marshall, 'It is emphatically the province and duty of the judicial department to say what the law is.' No amount of deference to judicial restraint can discharge this obligation." *People v. Summit*, 517 P.2d 850 (1974) 855 (Lee J., dissenting)

Indeed, it is small wonder that such a suggestion would come from the *Mallan* majority. The justices belong to that percentage of the populace who are the least keen to face reality, and so it is only natural that they would come up with such a scheme. To thinking people, however, it is nothing but a ploy to escape responsibility for their actions. To maintain a façade of respectability, it is easy to understand why they would want this change of policy to be so slow that no one really is held responsible for crimes against humanity. Even so, this is no good reason for dissolving the drug war effort over a period of decades. The price of appealing to vanity is bought at the expense of untold human misery, and there can be no justice, no rule of law, before this charade is put to an end.

4

SUMMARY

"The War on Drugs violates the fundamental common law principle of responsibility in its reliance on coercive, preventive laws—prohibition—passed in anticipation of misconduct, whether or not it actually occurs. It thus proceeds from a platform of disrespect for the idea of individual rights and responsibilities; its premises do not harmonize with those of the legal and political systems, and that dissonance may explain much of its futility and destructiveness."[303]

—Steven Wisotsky—

THIS CASE STUDY HAS exposed the American system of arbitrary law for what it is. It has also explored the qualitative difference between principled and unprincipled reasoning, and the problem with the latter has been made sufficiently clear. Hence, there is no reason to elaborate. Instead, what we shall do in this summary is to give the advocates of principled reasoning their due. I shall build on the analysis of the FC/NC Model, and in looking at the history of drug law challenges, little more than a handful of justices qualify for this noble status. Justices Abe, Levinson, Kobayashi, and the second Levinson of the Hawaii Supreme Court all passed with flying

---

[303] WISOTSKY, *BEYOND THE WAR ON DRUGS* (1990) 201

colors.[304] This honor also goes to Justices Kavanagh of the Michigan Supreme Court[305] and Sanders of the Washington Supreme Court.[306]

In Sanders's case, the issue before the court concerned a right to medical marijuana. However, I have taken the liberty of presuming that he would have applied the same reasoning in matters concerning recreational use. This may not be the case, but his opinion fulfills the necessary criteria. Justices Dolliver, Hicks, and Williams of the same court also voiced an opinion that qualifies,[307] and the same goes for Justices Seiler and Shangler of the Michigan Supreme Court.[308] I will also name Justice Adkins of the Florida Supreme Court for his dissenting opinions. He does, after all, establish that drug use is a protected privacy right,[309] and that the state must have more than a hypothetical rational basis" for its classification. He is clear that there must be a "valid and substantial reason for classifications,"[310] and assuming that he applies the same reasoning consistently, he deserves credit.

In addition to this, there are a few majority opinions that more or less qualify. In *English v. Miller*,[311] *People v.*

---

[304] *State v. Kantner,* 53 Haw. 327, 493 P.2d 306 (1972); *State v. Baker*, 56 Haw. 271, 535 P.2d 1394 (1975); *State v. Mallan*, 86 Haw. 440, 950 P.2d 178 (1998)

[305] *People v. Lorentzen*, 194 N.W.2d 827 (1972); *People v. Sinclair*, 387 Mich. 91, 194 N.W.2d 878 (1972)

[306] *Seeley v. State*, 132 Wash. 2d 776, 940 P.2d 604 (1997)

[307] *State v. Smith*, 610 P.2d 869, 93 Wn.2d 329 (1980)

[308] *State v. Mitchell*, 563 S.W.2d 18 (Mo. 1978)

[309] *Laird v. State*, 342 So.2d 962 (Fla. 1977) (Adkins J. dissenting)

[310] *Bourassa v. State*, 366 So. 2d 12 (Fla. 1978)

[311] 341 F. Supp. 714 (E.D. Va. 1972)

McCabe,[312] *People v. Sinclair*,[313] *Sam v. State*,[314] and *State v. Zornes*,[315] the court had sufficient integrity to invalidate the marijuana laws on equal protection grounds. However, as the issue before the court was whether the classification of marijuana together with opiates violated the equal protection clause, I believe that these justices would fail the test when push came to shove. Had the appellants raised the bigger issue, whether the different treatment of marijuana and alcohol users violated the equal protection clause, they would most likely, just as every other court faced with this issue, have denied protection on equal protection grounds and so I do not want to reward them with FC status. There are also the justices at the Alaska Supreme Court who, with *Ravin,* found marijuana use to be a protected privacy right and demanded that the state justify its prohibition. Thus, they deserve credit, but the reasoning of the court was so entrenched in the NC paradigm that no FC status shall be awarded.

In addition to the justices summarized, we can add a few from the lower courts. Even so, it is a rather sorry spectacle. We are dealing with more than a hundred constitutional challenges and so we can assume that 90 percent of American justices belong to the NC category. That is, they may from time to time expound the kind of principled reasoning needed to fulfill FC criteria in other areas, but this is easy. It is in the hard cases (as in constitutional challenges to the prohibitions on drugs and prostitution) that they have an opportunity to prove their qualities, and here they fall short. Again and again, we find their reasoning too contaminated by the

---

[312] 49 Ill. 2d 338, 275 N.E.2d 407 (1971)

[313] 387 Mich. 91, 194 N.W.2d 878 (1972)

[314] 500 P.2d 291 (Okl.Cr.App.)

[315] 78 Wash. 2d 9, 475 P.2d 109

cultural prejudice of the status quo to correctly apply first principles.

We can also look for the same traits among other legal scholars, such as professors of law. Here the record is also flimsy, but it is unlikely that more than 10 percent will qualify for FC status. All things being equal, this is what we can expect from the general population and I have seen no indication that FC traits are more common among academics. However, even if this should be the case generally speaking, the trend among Ninth Amendment scholars is reversed. Looking at their scholarship, 90 percent could classify as FC individuals. Hence, there is hope for the future. These are the scholars with the firmest grip on constitutional interpretation, and had they been consulted—and their knowledge applied— the American legal system would evolve into FC status.

If we want to get the American system back on track, we need only listen to these individuals. They are the avant-garde, the harbingers of things to come, but they are mostly talking to themselves and have little influence on current events. At the very least, the justices at the U.S. Supreme Court do not seem to have much regard for their criticisms. Just like most politicians, prosecutors, and career bureaucrats at the Justice Department, they remain dedicated to doctrines of arbitrary law and their foremost concern seems to be keeping the status quo intact.

This, again, is as one can expect. As Professor Ervin Staub noted, "being part of a system shapes views, rewards adherence to dominant views, and makes deviation psychologically demanding and difficult."[316] Hence, as the dominant view is the NC mindset, they are representative of

---

[316] ZIMBARDO, *THE LUCIFER EFFECT* (2009) 286. See also ERVIN STAUB, *THE ROOTS OF EVIL: THE ORIGINS OF GENOCIDE AND OTHER GROUP VIOLENCE*

this perspective and it comes as no surprise that they have ignored principled reasoning. It is all part of the pattern, and we can expect our body of law to remain in shambles for quite some time, as the system's force of inertia will continue to fight integrity and FC reasoning every step of the way, while the majority of the population remains oblivious.

Even so, we can expect the NC mindset to lose out in the end. As documented in *To Right a Wrong*, we are in the midst of a paradigm shift and the only question is how expensive the funeral will be in terms of lives needlessly lost, millions wrongfully incarcerated, and money unwisely spent promoting organized crime and feeding the totalitarian aspects of the state. The stakes are high. Every year this war continues, the body count and human misery that follows in its wake is comparable to that of conventional wars; as much as 400.000 lives are unnecessarily lost, and one day we will look back and remember the Drug War as one of history's most heinous crimes against humanity.

While prohibitionists will disagree, the evidence is overwhelming. As we have seen, the case against drug prohibition is nearing complete; every aspect of its unconstitutionality has been documented and the problems with the prohibition argument have been exposed in full detail. More and more people are catching up, and it is only a matter of time before prohibitionists will have to recognize our right to an effective remedy.

The longer until they do, the more profound will be their denial of responsibility, and the more our officials will go from a position of embarrassment to criminal negligence. To the extent they continue to ignore the evidence, they are depriving the people of basic constitutional rights, and they are, as openly as civil servants ever can be expected to, saying

F.U. to the people they are supposed to serve. No one of sound mind would vote for officials such as these and no officials worthy of the people's trust will let this state of affairs continue unchecked. Hence, to the extent that our officials take their duties seriously, they will assist us in ending drug prohibition.

Also, to the extent that the NC doctrines discussed are a sincere attempt to find the best possible instruments for anchoring the light of first principles, of de-abstracting and transfusing it into a more pliable and concrete form (i.e., something to work with), we can expect judges and lawyers to embrace FC doctrines as soon as their pre-eminence is established. This, no doubt, is the situation today. Indeed, the case for a systemic recalibration towards a state of resonance with principled law is so powerful that impeachment procedures will be the only proper response if the courts fails the people.

This should be uncontroversial. As Professor Gerber noted, "[t]he theory of the Constitution requires that Congress exercise the political courage necessary to perform its constitutional duty of impeaching those justices who seek to 'rewrite' the Constitution rather than interpret it."[317] This is what most justices have done to this day. Under the cover of "objectivity" the courts have never been more subjectively driven,[318] and the flawed reasoning by which they operate

---

[317] Gerber, *Liberal Originalism* (2014) 22

[318] "The underlying rationale for choosing selected liberties to be protected from government interference while leaving the rest largely unprotected is to inform us clearly that the Court exercises 'the utmost care whenever asked to break new ground in this field, lest the liberty protected by the Due Process Clause be subtly transformed into the policy preferences of the Members of this Court.' In actuality, however, this has not restrained the Court. Judicial preferences, masked by a glossary of shibboleths, have taken from us the original, rational system of determining whether a governmental restriction bears a substantial relation to the

ensures the unnecessary, illegitimate, and continued suffering of millions. To the extent the judiciary continues this travesty, they are unlawfully depriving the people of their constitutional rights, and such open hostility is not what the founders intended.

All things considered, therefore, unless representatives quickly turn things around, Americans will have right to declare the government an enemy of the people and abolish that apparatus which has become so destructive to the principles and ends of the founding. To say this is neither anarchistic hyperbole nor aggravating hate speech: It is simply the idea of America. It should be uncontroversial that American officials are responsible to the people, and that, when betraying their trust, the consequences shall be proportional to their treason. Self-serving, conniving, and dishonest officials should by all rights be fearful of the people to whom they are beholden—and just like America was an idea whose time had come 250 years ago, so it is time for Americans to embrace the ideas of the Founding.

---

police power." Preiser, *Rediscovering a Coherent Rationale for Substantive Due Process* (2003) 11

APPENDIX

CONSTITUTIONAL CHALLENGES TO THE DRUG LAW

Blincoe v. State, 204 S.E.2d 597 (Ga. 1974)

Borras v. State, 229 So. 2d 244 (Fla. 1969)

Boswell v. State, 290 Ala. 349, 276 o. 2d 592, 596[5] (1973)

Bourassa v. State, 366 So. 2d 12 (Fla. 1978)

Commonwealth v. Leis, 355 Mass. 189, 243 N.E.2d 898 (1969)

Daut v. United States, 405 F.2d 312 (9th Cir. 1968), cert. denied, 402 U.S. 945, 91 S.Ct. 1624, 29 L.Ed.2d 114 (1971)

Egan v. Sheriff, Clark County, 88 Nev. 611,503 P.2d 16 (1972);

English v. Miller, 341 F. Supp. 714 (E.D.Va.1972)

English v. Virginia Probation and Parole Bd., 481 F.2d 188 (4 Cir. 1973)

Gaskin v. State, 490 S.W.2d 521 (Tenn. 1973), appeal dismissed, 414 U.S. 886, 94 S.Ct. 221, 38 L.Ed.2d 133 (1973)

Gonzales v. Raich, 545 U.S. 1, 125 S.Ct. 2195, 162 L.Ed.2d 1 (2005)

Gonzales v. State, 373 S.W.2d 249 (Tex. Crim. App. 1963)

Gray v. State, 525 P.2d 524, (Alaska 1974)

Hamilton v. State, 366 So. 2d 8 (Fla. 1979)

Harmash v. United States, 414 U.S. 831, 94 S.Ct. 165, 38 L.Ed.2d 65 (1973)

Harmelin v. Michigan, 501 U.S. 957 (1991)

Illinois NORML v. Scott, 383 N.E.2d 1330, 66 Ill. App.3d 633 (1978)

Joslin v. 14th District Judge, 76 Mich. App. 90,255 N.W.2d 782 (1977)

Kehrli v. Sprinkle, 524 F.2d 328 (10 Cir. 1975), certiorari denied, 426 U.S. 947, 96 S.Ct. 3165,49 L.Ed.2d 1183 (1976)

Kenny v. State, 51 Ala. App. 35,282 So.2d 387, certiorari denied, 291 Ala. 786, 282 So.2d 392 (1973)

Kreisher v. State, 319 A.2d 31 (Del. 1974)

Kuromiya v. United States, 37 F. Supp. 2d 717 (E.D. Pa. 1999)

Laird v. State, 342 So.2d 962 (Fla. 1977)

Leary v. United States, 383 F.2d 851 (5th Cir. 1967), rev'd on other grounds, 395 U.S. 6, 89 S.Ct. 1532, 23 L.Ed.2d 57 (1969)

Louisiana Af. of Nat. Or. for Ref. of Marijuana Laws v. Guste, 380 F. Supp. 404 (E.D. La. 1974), affd mem., 511 F.2d 1400 (5th Cir. 1975), cert. denied, 96 S. Ct. 129 (1975).

Marcoux v Attorney General, 375 N.E.2d 688 (Mass. 1978)

Miller v. State, 458 S.W.2d 680 (Tex.Cr.App. 1970)

Nat'l Org. for Reform of Marijuana Laws (NORML) v. Bell, 488 F. Supp. 123 (D.D.C. 1980)

Oliver v. Udall, 113 U.S.App. D.C. 212, 306 F.2d 819, cert. denied, 372 U.S. 908, 83 S. Ct. 720, 9 L. Ed. 2d 717 (1962).

People v. Aguiar, 257 Cal. App. 2d 597, 65 Cal. Rptr. 171, cert. denied, 393 U.S. 970, 89 S. Ct. 411, 21 L. Ed. 2d 383 (1968)

People v. Alexander, 56 Mich. App. 400, 223 N.W.2d 750 (1974)

People v. Bloom, 270 Cal.App.2d 731, 76 Cal.Rptr. 137 (1969)

People v. Bourg, 552 P.2d 504 (1976)

People v Demers, 42 App Div 2d 634; 345 N.Y.S.2d 184 (1973)

People v. Lorentzen, 387 Mich. 167, 194 N.W.2d 827(1972)

People v. McCabe, 49 Ill. 2d 338, 275 N.E.2d 407 (1971)

People v. McCaffrey, 29 Ill. App.3d 1088,332 N.E.2d 28 (1975)

People v. Morehouse, 80 Misc.2d 406, 364 N.Y.S.2d 108 (Sup.Ct. 1975)

People v. Schmidt, 272 N.W.2d 732 (Ct.App. Mich. 1978)

People v. Sheridan, 271 Cal. App. 2d 429, 76 Cal. Rptr. 655 (1969)

People v. Sinclair, 387 Mich. 91, 194 N.W.2d 878 (1972)

People v. Stark, 157 Colo. 59, 400 P.2d 923 (1965)

People v. Summit, 517 P.2d 850 (Colo. 1974)

People v. Walton, 116 Ill. App.2d 293 (1969)

People v. Woody, 61 Cal. 2d 716, 40 Cal. Rptr. 69, 394 P.2d 813 (1964)

Raich v. Gonzales, 500 F.3d 850 (9th Cir. 2007)

Raines v. State, 225 So. 2d 330 (Fla. 1969)

Ravin v. State, 537 P.2d 494 (Alaska 1975)

Ross v. State, 360 N.E.2d 1015 (Ct.App. Ind. 1977)

Sam v. State, 500 P.2d 291 (Okl.Cr.1972)

Seeley v. State, 132 Wash. 2d 776, 940 P.2d 604 (1997)

Spence v. Sachs, 173 Ohio St. 419, 183 N.E.2d 363

State Rel. Scott v. Conaty, 187 S.E.2d 119 (1972)

State v. Anderson, **558 P.2d 307**(Wash. Ct. App. 1976)

State v. Anonymous, 32 Conn. Supp. 324, 355 A.2d 729 (1976)

State v. Baker, 56 Haw. 271, 535 P.2d 1394 (1975)

State v. Carus, 118 N.J.Super. 159, 286 A.2d 740 (1972)

State v Donovan, 344 A.2d 401 (Me, 1975)

State v. Ennis, 334 N.W.2d 827 (N.D.), cert. denied, U.S. 104 S. Ct. 484 (1983)

State v. Hanson, 364 N.W.2d 786 (Minn. 1985)

State v Infante, 199 Neb. 601; 260 N.W.2d 323 (1977)

State v. Kantner, 53 Haw. 327, 493 P.2d 306, cert. denied, 409 U.S. 948 (1972)

State v Kaplan, 23 N.C. App. 410; 209 S.E.2d 325 (1974)

State v. Kells, 259 N.W.2d 19 (Neb. 1977)

State v. Leins, 234 N.W.2d 645 (Iowa 1975)

State v Leppanen, 252 Or. 352; 449 P.2d 447 (1969)

State v. Mallan, 950 P.2d 178 (1998)

State v. Mitchell, 563 S.W.2d 18 (Mo. 1978) (en banc)

State v Murphy, 117 Ariz. 57,570 P.2d 1070 (1977)

State v. Nugent, 125 N.J. Super. 528, 312 A.2d 158 (1973)

State v O'Bryan, 96 Idaho 548; 531 P.2d 1193 (1975),

State v. Olson, 127 Wis. 2d 412, 380 N.W.2d 375 (1985)

State v. Rao, 171 Conn. 600, 370 A.2d 1310 (1976)

State v. Renfro, 56 Haw. 501, 542 P.2d 366 (1975)

State v. Sliger, 261 La. 999, 261 So.2d 643 (1972)

State v. Smith, 93 Wn.2d 329, 610 P.2d 869 (1980)

State v. Stallman, 673 S.W.2d 857 (Ct.App. Mo. 1984)

State v. Stock, 463 S.W.2d 889 (Mo. 1971)

State v. Strong, 245 N.W.2d 277 (S.D. 1976)

State v Tabory, 260 S.C. 355; 196 S.E.2d 111 (1973)

State v. Zornes, 78 Wash. 2d 9, 469 P.2d 552 (banc 1970)

State v. Wadsworth, 109 Ariz. 59, 505 P.2d 230, (banc 1973)

State v. Weidner, 47 Wis. 2d 321, 177 N.W.2d 69 (1970)

State v. White, 153 Mont. 193, 456 P.2d 54 (1969)

State v. Whitney, 637 P.2d 956 (Wash. 1981) (en banc)

United States v. Aguilar, 883 F.2d 662, 692 (9th Cir. 1989)

United States v. Bergdoll, 412 F. Supp. 1308 (D. Del. 1976)

United States v. Castro, 401 F. Supp. 120 (N.D. Ill. 1975)

United States v. Drotar, 416 F.2d 914 (5th Cir. 1969), vacated on other grounds, 402 U.S. 939, 91 S.Ct. 1628, 29 L.Ed.2d 107 (1971)

United States v. Eramdjian, (S.D. Cal. 1957), 155 F. Supp. 914 (S.D. Cal. 1957)

United States v. Fogarty, 692 F.2d 542 (8th Cir. 1982), cert. denied, 460 U.S. 1040 (1983)

United States v. Fry, 787 F.2d 903 (4th Cir. 1986)

United States v. Gaertner, 583 F.2d 308, 312 (7th Cir.1978) (per curiam)

United States v. Gramlich, 551 F.2d 1359 (5 Cir. 1977), certiorari denied, 434 U.S. 866, 98 S.Ct. 201,54 L.Ed.2d 141 (1977)

United States v. Greene, 892 F.2d 453, 456 (6th Cir. 1989)

United States v. Horsley, 519 F.2d 1264 (5th Cir. 1975)

United States v. Kiffer, 477 F.2d 349 (2d Cir.), cert. denied, 414 U.S. 831, 94 S.Ct. 62, 38 L.Ed.2d 65 (1973)

United States v. LaFroscia, 354 F. Supp. 1338 (S.D.N.Y. 1973)

United States v. Maas, 551 F. Supp. 645 (D.N.J. 1982)

United States v. Maiden, 355 F.Supp. 743, 749 (D.Conn.1973)

United States v. Middleton, 690 F.2d 820 (11th Cir. 1982), cert. denied, 460 U.S. 1051 (1983)

United States v. Miroyan, 577 F.2d 489 (9th Cir.), cert. denied, 439 U.S. 896 (1978)

United States v. Oakland Cannabis Buyers' Cooperative, 190 F.3d 1109 (9th Cir. 1999)

United States v. Pickard, et. al., No. 2:11-CR-0449-KJM (2015)

United States v. Pineda-Moreno, 688 F.3d 1087 (9th Cir. 2012)

United States v. Rodriquez-Comacho, 468 F.2d 1220 (9th Cir. 1972), cert. denied, 410 U.S. 985, 93 S.Ct. 1512, 36 L.Ed.2d 182 (1973)

United States v. Rogers, 549 F.2d 107 (1976)

United States v. Thorne, 325 A.2d 764 (1974)

United States v. Ward, 387 F.2d 843 (7th Cir. 1967)

United States v. Washington, 887 F.Supp.2d 1077, 1103 (D. Mont. 2012)

United States v. White Plume, 447 F.3d 1067 (2005)

Wolkind v. Selph, 495 F.Supp. 507, 513 (D.Va.1980), aff'd, 649 F.2d 865 (4th Cir. 1981)

LIST OF FC DISSENTERS

Bourassa v. State, 366 So. 2d 12 (Fla. 1978). (Adkins J., dissenting)

Hamilton v. State, 366 So. 2d 8 (1978) (Adkins J., dissenting)

Laird v. State, 342 So.2d 962 (Fla. 1977) (Adkins J., dissenting) (Not fully FC but establishes that drug use is a protected privacy right)

People v. Lorentzen, 194 N.W.2d 827 (1972) 182 (Kavanagh J., concurring in part, dissenting in part)

People v. Sinclair, 387 Mich. 91, 194 N.W.2d 878 (1972) (Kavanagh J., concurring)

State v. Baker, 56 Haw. 271, 535 P.2d 1394 (1975) (Kobayashi J., dissenting)

State v. Kantner, 53Haw. 327, 493 P.2d 306 (1972) 311-20 (JJ. Abe, Levinson, and Kobayashi dissenting)

State v. Mallan, 86 Haw. 440, 950 P.2d 178 (1998) (Levinson J., dissenting)

State v. Mitchell, 563 S.W.2d 18 (Mo. 1978) 28-37 (Seiler J. and Shangler Sp.J., dissenting)

State v. Smith, 610 P.2d 869, 93 Wn.2d 329 (1980) 355-367 (Dolliver J., dissenting)

Seeley v. State, 132 Wash. 2d 776, 940 P.2d 604 (1997) (Sanders J., dissenting)

BIBLIOGRAPHY

Ahrens, Deborah, *Drug Panics in the Twenty-First Century: Ecstasy, Prescription Drugs, and the Reframing of the War on Drugs*, ALBANY GOVERNMENT LAW REVIEW Vol. 6:397 (2013)

ALEXANDER, MICHELLE, *THE NEW JIM CROW: MASS INCARCERATION IN THE AGE OF COLORBLINDNESS* (New Press 2011)

Alexandre, Michelle, *Sex, Drugs, Rock & Roll and Moral Dirgisme: Toward a Reformation of Drug and Prostitution Regulations*, UMKC LAW REVIEW Vol. 78, No. 1 (2009)

ALEXY, ROBERT, *A THEORY OF CONSTITUTIONAL RIGHTS* (Oxford 2002)

Alexy, Robert, *Constitutional Rights and Proportionality*, JOURNAL FOR CONSTITUTIONAL THEORY AND PHILOSOPHY OF LAW VOL. 22:51 (2014)

AKHIL REED AMAR, *AMERICA'S UNWRITTEN CONSTITUTION: THE PRECEDENTS AND PRINCIPLES WE LIVE BY* (Basic Books 2012)

Anderson & Rees, *The Legalization of Recreational Marijuana: How Likely Is the Worst-Case Scenario?* JOURNAL OF POLICY ANALYSIS AND MANAGEMENT Vol. 33:221 (2014)

ANDREWS, ANDY, *HOW DO YOU KILL 11 MILLION PEOPLE* (Thomas Nelson 2010)

Araiza, William D., *Deference to Congressional Fact-Finding in Rights-Enforcing and Rights-Limiting Legislation*, NYU LAW REVIEW Vol. 88:878 (2013)

ARKES, HADLEY, *BEYOND THE CONSTITUTION* (Princeton 1990)

ARKES, HADLEY, *CONSTITUTIONAL ILLUSIONS & ANCHORING TRUTHS: THE TOUCHSTONE OF THE NATURAL LAW* (Cambridge 2010)

Ashworth, Andrew, *Is the Criminal Law a Lost Cause?* LAW QUARTERLY REVIEW Vol.116:225 (2000)

BAILYN, BERNARD, *THE IDEOLOGICAL ORIGINS OF THE AMERICAN REVOLUTION* (Harvard 1967)

BAKALAR, JAMES B. & GRINSPOON, LESTER, *DRUG CONTROL IN A FREE SOCIETY*, (Cambridge 1998)

Balkin, Jack M., *Abortion and Original Meaning*, CONSTITUTIONAL COMMENTARY Vol. 24:291 (2007)

Ball, Carlos A., *Why Liberty Judicial Review is as Legitimate as Equality Review: The Case of Gay Rights Jurisprudence*, JOURNAL OF CONSTITUTIONAL LAW Vol. 14:1 (2011)

Bandow, Doug, *From Fighting the Drug War to Protecting the Right to Use Drugs: Recognizing a Forgotten Liberty*, FRASER INSTITUTE (2012)

Baradaran, Shima, *Drugs and Violence,* UNIVERSITY OF UTAH COLLEGE OF LAW Research Paper No. 75 (2015)

Barnett, Randy E., *An Originalism for Nonoriginalists*, BOSTON UNIVERSITY SCHOOL OF LAW Working Paper No. 99-14 (1999)

Barnett, Randy, *Bad Trip: Drug Prohibition and the Weakness of Public Policy*, YALE LAW JOURNAL Vol. 103:2593 (1994)

Barnett, Randy E., *Constitutional Clichés*, CAPITAL UNIVERSITY LAW REVIEW Vol. 36:493 (2008)

Barnett, Randy E., *From Antislavery Lawyer to Chief Justice: The Remarkable but Forgotten Career of Salmon P. Chase*, CASE WESTERN RESERVE LAW REVIEW Vol. 63:653 (2013)

Barnett, Randy E., *The Golden Mean Between Kurt & Dan: A Moderate Reading of the Ninth Amendment*, DRAKE LAW REVIEW Vol. 56:897 (2008)

Barnett, Randy E., *The Gravitational Force of Originalism*, GEORGETOWN PUBLIC LAW AND LEGAL THEORY Research Paper No. 13-010 (2013)

Barnett, Randy E., *The Harmful Side Effects of Drug Prohibition*, UTAH LAW REVIEW 11-34 (2009)

Barnett, Randy E., *The Imperative of Natural Rights in Today's World*, BOSTON UNIVERSITY SCHOOL OF LAW, Working Paper No. 03-20 (2003)

Barnett, Randy E., *Is the Constitution Libertarian?* GEORGETOWN PUBLIC LAW Research Paper No. 1432854 (2008)

Barnett, Randy E., *Justice Kennedy's Libertarian Revolution: Lawrence v. Texas*, BOSTON UNIVERSITY SCHOOL OF LAW, Working Paper No. 03-13 (2003)

Barnett, Randy E., *The Misconceived Assumption about Constitutional Assumptions*, GEORGETOWN LAW FACULTY Working Papers (2008)

Barnett, Randy E., *The Ninth Amendment: It Means What It Says*, TEXAS LAW REVIEW Vol. 85:1 (2006)

Barnett, Randy E., *The Original Meaning of the Judicial Power*, BOSTON UNIVERSITY SCHOOL OF LAW Working Paper No. 03-18 (2003)

Barnett, Randy E., *The Original Meaning of the Necessary and Proper Clause*, BOSTON UNIVERSITY SCHOOL OF LAW Working Paper No. 03-11 (2003)

Barnett, Randy E., *The People or the State: Chrisholm v. Georgia and Popular Sovereignty* VIRGINIA LAW REVIEW Vol. 93 (2007)

Barnett, Randy E., *The Presumption of Liberty and the Public Interest: Medical Marijuana and Fundamental Rights*, WASHINGTON UNIVERSITY JOURNAL OF LAW AND POLICY Vol. 22:29 (2006)

Barnett, Randy E., *The Proper Scope of the Police Power*, NOTRE DAME LAW REVIEW Vol. 79:429 (2004)

BARNETT, RANDY E., *RESTORING THE LOST CONSTITUTION: THE PRESUMPTION OF LIBERTY* (Princeton 2014)

Barnett, Randy E., *Scrutiny Land*, MICHIGAN LAW REVIEW Vol. 106:1479 (2008)

BARNETT, RANDY E., *THE STRUCTURE OF LIBERTY: JUSTICE AND THE RULE OF LAW* (Oxford 2014)

Barnett, Randy E., *We the People: Each and Every One*, YALE LAW JOURNAL Vol. 123:2576 (2014)

Barnett, Randy E., *Who's Afraid of Unenumerated Rights?* JOURNAL OF CONSTITUTIONAL LAW Vol. 9:1 (2006)

Barrett, Damon, *Security, Development and Human Rights: Normative, Legal and Policy Challenges for the International Drug Control System*, INTERNATIONAL JOURNAL OF DRUG POLICY 21 (2010)

BAUM, DAN, *SMOKE AND MIRRORS: THE WAR ON DRUGS AND THE POLITICS OF FAILURE* (Little Brown 1996)

Beale, Sara Sun, *What's Law Got To Do With It? The Political, Social, Psychological and Other Non-Legal Factors Influencing the Development of (Federal) Criminal Law*, BUFFALO CRIMINAL LAW REVIEW Vol. 1:23 (1997)

BEATTY, DAVID M., *THE ULTIMATE RULE OF LAW* (Oxford 2004)

BECKER, DEAN, *TO END THE WAR ON DRUGS: POLICYMAKERS' EDITION* (DTN Media 2014)

Benson, Bruce L., *The War on Drugs: A Public Bad*, NORTHWESTERN UNIVERSITY'S SEARLE CENTER ON LAW (2008)

Bergland, David, *Libertarianism, Natural Rights and the Constitution, A Commentary on Recent Libertarian Literature*, CLEVELAND STATE LAW REVIEW Vol. 44:499 (1996)

BERTRAM, EVA, ET AL., *DRUG WAR POLITICS: THE PRICE OF DENIAL* (University of California 1996)

BEWLEY-TAYLOR, DAVID R.., *INTERNATIONAL DRUG CONTROL: CONSENSUS FRACTURED* (Cambridge 2012)

Bibas, Stephanos & Bierschbach, Richard A., *Constitutionally Tailoring Punishment*, MICHIGAN LAW REVIEW Vol. 112:397 (2013)

Bilionis, Louis D., *The New Scrutiny*, Emory Law Journal Vol. 51:101 (2002)

Bilionis, Louis D., *On the Significance of Constitutional Spirit*, NORTH CAROLINA LAW REVIEW Vol. 70:1803 (1992)

Bilionis, Louis D., *Process, the Constitution, and Substantive Criminal Law*, MICHIGAN LAW REVIEW Vol.96:1269 (1998)

BLACK, CHARLES L., *A NEW BIRTH FOR FREEDOM: HUMAN RIGHTS, NAMED AND UNNAMED* (Yale 1999)

BLAU, JUDITH & MONCADA, ALBERTO, *JUSTICE IN THE UNITED STATES: HUMAN RIGHTS AND THE U.S. CONSTITUTION* (Rowman & Littlefield 2006)

Blickman & Jelsma, *Drug Policy Reform in Practice: Experiences with Alternatives in Europe and the US*, TRANSNATIONAL INSTITUTE (2009)

Block, Walter, *Drug Prohibition: A Legal and Economic Analysis*, JOURNAL OF BUSINESS ETHICS Vol. 12:689 (1993)

Blumenson, Eric, *Recovering from Drugs and the Drug War: An Achievable Public Health Alternative*, JOURNAL OF GENDER, RACE AND JUSTICE Vol. 6, No. 2 (2002)

Blumenson, Eric & Nilsen, Eva, *Policing for Profit: The Drug War's Hidden Economic Agenda*, UNIVERSITY OF CHICAGO LAW REVIEW Vol. 65:35 (1998)

BOLLINGER, LORENTZ (ED.), *CANNABIS SCIENCE: FROM PROHIBITION TO HUMAN RIGHT* (Peter Lang 1997)

Bollinger, Lorentz, *Recent Developments Regarding Drug Law and Policy in Germany and the European Community: The Evolution of Drug Control in Europe*, JOURNAL OF DRUG ISSUES (2002)

Bomhoff, Jacco, *Genealogies of Balancing as Discourse*, LAW & ETHICS OF HUMAN RIGHTS, Vol. 4, Issue 1, Article 6 (2010)

Bonnie, Richard & Whitebread, Charles, *The Forbidden Fruit and the Tree of Knowledge: An Inquiry into the Legal History of American Marijuana Prohibition*, VIRGINIA LAW REVIEW Vol. 56:971 (1970)

Borgmann, Caitlin E., *Rethinking Judicial Deference to Legislative Fact-Finding*, INDIANA LAW JOURNAL Vol. 81:1 (2009)

BOWARD, JAMES, *LOST RIGHTS: THE DESTRUCTION OF AMERICAN LIBERTY* (St. Martin's Griffin 1995)

Boyd, Graham, *Collateral Damage in the War on Drugs*, VILLANOVA LAW REVIEW Vol. 47:839 (2002)

Brandeis, Jason, *The Continuing Vitality of Ravin v. State: Alaskans Still Have a Constitutional Right to Possess Marijuana in the Privacy of their Homes*, ALASKA LAW REVIEW Vol. 29:2 (2012)

Brashear, Bruce, *Marijuana Prohibition and the Constitutional Right of Privacy: An Examination of Ravin v. State*, TULSA LAW JOURNAL Vol. 11:563 (1975)

Brown, Darryl K., *Can Criminal Law Be Controlled?* MICHIGAN LAW REVIEW Vol. 108:971 (2010)

Brown-Nagin, Tomiko, *The Civil Rights Canon: Above and Below*, YALE LAW JOURNAL Vol. 123:2698 (2014)

Brown, Rebecca L., *Liberty, the New Equality*, NYU LAW REVIEW Vol. 77:1491 (2002)

Buchhandler-Raphael, Michal, *Drugs, Dignity, and Danger: Human Dignity as a Constitutional Constraint to Limit Overcriminalization*, TENNESSEE LAW REVIEW, Vol. 80 (2013)

BURDICK, CHARLES K., *THE LAW OF THE AMERICAN CONSTITUTION: ITS ORIGIN AND DEVELOPMENT* (Putnam 1922)

Chemerinsky, Erwin, *The Constitution and Punishment*, STANFORD LAW REVIEW Vol. 56:1049 (2004)

Chemerinsky, Erwin, *Substantive Due Process*, TOURO LAW REVIEW Vol. 15:1501 (1999)

Christiansen, Matthew A., *A Great Schism: Social Norms and Marijuana Prohibition*, HARVARD LAW & POLICY REVIEW Vol. 4:229 (2010)

Colb, Sherry, *Freedom from Incarceration: Why is This Right Different from All Other Rights?* NYU LAW REVIEW Vol. 69:781 (1994)

Cole, David, *Formalism, Realism, and the War on Drugs*, SUFFOLK UNIVERSITY LAW REVIEW Vol. 35: 241 (2001)

Conkle, Daniel O., *The Second Death of Substantive Due Process*, INDIANA LAW JOURNAL Vol. 62:215 (1987)

CONRAD, CLAY S., *JURY NULLIFICATION: THE EVOLUTION OF A DOCTRINE* (Carolina 1998)

CONRAD, NORRIS & RESNER, *HUMAN RIGHTS AND THE US DRUG WAR* (Creative Xpressions 2001)

Csete, Joanne, *From the Mountaintops: What the World Can Learn from Drug Policy Change in Switzerland*, OPEN SOCIETY FOUNDATIONS (2010)

Cunnings, Jordan, *Nonserious Marijuana Offenses and Noncitizens: Uncounseled Pleas and Disproportionate Consequences*, UCLA LAW REVIEW Vol. 62:510 (2015)

CURTIS, MICHAEL, *NO STATE SHALL ABRIDGE: THE FOURTEENTH AMENDMENT AND THE BILL OF RIGHTS* (Duke 1986)

D'Amato, Anthony, *Natural Law: A Libertarian View*, FACULTY WORKING PAPERS, Paper 148 (2008)

Danovitch, Itai, *Sorting Through the Science on Marijuana: Facts, Fallacies, and Implications for Legalization*, MCGEORGE LAW REVIEW Vol. 43:91 (2013)

DE GREIFF, PABLO (ED.), *DRUGS AND THE LIMITS OF LIBERALISM* (Cornell 1999)

Dichter, Mark S., *Marijuana and the Law: The Constitutional Challenges to Marijuana Laws in Light of the Social Aspects of Marijuana Use*, VILLANOVA LAW REVIEW Vol. 13:851 (1968)

Dippel, Horst, *Modern Constitutionalism: An Introduction to a History in the Need of Writing*, THE LEGAL HISTORY REVIEW Vol. 73:153 (2005)

Domosławski, Artur, *Drug Policy in Portugal: The Benefits of Decriminalizing Drug Use*, OPEN SOCIETY FOUNDATIONS (2011)

Doss, Arden & Doss, Diane, *On Morals, Privacy, and the Constitution*, UNIVERSITY OF MIAMI LAW REVIEW Vol. 25:395 (1971)

Dubber, Markus D., *A Political Theory of Criminal Law: Autonomy and the Legitimacy of State Punishment*, LEGITIMATING CRIMINAL LAW (2004)

Dubber, Markus D., *The Legality Principle in American and German Criminal Law: An Essay in Comparative Legal History* (2010)

Dubber, Markus D., *New Legal Science: Toward Law as a Global Discipline* (2014)

Dubber, Markus D., *The New Police Science and the Police Power Model of the Criminal Process* (2004)

Dubber, Markus D., *Policing Possession: The War on Crime and the End of Criminal Law*, JOURNAL OF CRIMINAL LAW AND CRIMINOLOGY Vol. 91:829 (2001)

Dubber, Markus D., *Toward a Constitutional Law of Crime and Punishment*, HASTINGS LAW JOURNAL Vol. 55 (2004)

Duke, Steven B., *Drug Prohibition: an Unnatural Disaster*, FACULTY SCHOLARSHIP SERIES, paper 812 (1995)

Duke, Steven B., *The Future of Marijuana in the United States,* YALE LAW SCHOOL, Public Law Working Paper No. 299 (2013)

Duke, Steven B., *Mass Imprisonment, Crime Rates, and the Drug War: A Penological and Humanitarian Disgrace,* FACULTY SCHOLARSHIP SERIES, Paper 826 (2010)

DUKE, STEVEN, B. & CROSS, ALBERT C., *AMERICA'S LONGEST WAR: RETHINKING OUR TRAGIC CRUSADE AGAINST DRUGS* (Tarcher/Putnam 1993)

DWORKIN, RONALD, *A MATTER OF PRINCIPLE* (Harvard 1985)

DWORKIN, RONALD, *LAW'S EMPIRE* (Harvard 1986)

DWORKIN, RONALD, *SOVEREIGN VIRTUE: THE THEORY AND PRACTICE OF EQUALITY* (Harvard 2002)

DWORKIN, RONALD, *TAKING RIGHTS SERIOUSLY* (Harvard 1978)

Ely, John Hart, *Legislative and Administrative Motivation in Constitutional Law*, FACULTY SCHOLARSHIP SERIES, paper 4114 (1970)

EPSTEIN, EDWARD J., *AGENCY OF FEAR: OPIATES AND POLITICAL POWER IN AMERICA* (Verso 1990)

Erlinder, Peter, *Mens Rea, Due Process, and the Supreme Court: Toward a Constitutional Doctrine of Substantive Criminal Law*, AMERICAN JOURNAL OF CRIMINAL LAW Vol. 9:163 (1989)

ESCOHOTADO, ANTONIO, *A BRIEF HISTORY OF DRUGS: FROM THE STONE AGE TO THE STONED AGE* (Park Street 1999)

Eskridge, William N., *Destabilizing Due Process and Evolutive Equal Protection*, UCLA LAW REVIEW Vol. 47:1183 (2000)

European Commission for Democracy through Law, *European and U.S. Constitutionalism*, SCIENCE AND TECHNIQUE OF DEMOCRACY, No. 37 (2003)

Eylon & Harel, *The Right to Judicial Review,* VIRGINIA LAW REVIEW Vol. 92, No. 5 (2006)

Fallon, Richard H., *Individual Rights and Governmental Powers*, GEORGIA LAW REVIEW Vol. 27:343 (1993)

Fallon, Richard H., *Legitimacy and the Constitution*, HARVARD LAW REVIEW Vol. 118:1787 (2005)

Farrell, Robert C., *Justice Kennedy's Idiosyncratic Understanding of Equal Protection and Due Process, and its Costs*, QUINNIPIAC LAW REVIEW Vol. 32:439 (2014)

FEINBERG, JOEL, *HARMLESS WRONGDOING: THE MORAL LIMITS OF THE CRIMINAL LAW* (Oxford 1990)

FEINBERG, JOEL, *HARM TO OTHERS: THE MORAL LIMITS OF THE CRIMINAL LAW* (Oxford 1987)

Finer, Joel J., *Psychedelics and Religious Freedom*, HASTINGS LAW JOURNAL Vol. 19:667 (1968)

Finkelstein, Claire, *Positivism and the Notion of an Offense*, CALIFORNIA LAW REVIEW Vol. 88:335 (2000)

FISH, JEFFERSON (ED.), *HOW TO LEGALIZE DRUGS* (Northvale 1998)

Fiss, Owen M., *Groups and the Equal Protection Clause*, PHILOSOPHY AND PUBLIC AFFAIRS Vol. 5:107 (1976)

FORST, RAINER, *THE RIGHT TO JUSTIFICATION: A CONSTRUCTIVIST THEORY OF JUSTICE* (Columbia 2011)

FORTE, ROBERT (ED.), *ENTHEOGENS AND THE FUTURE OF RELIGION* (Park Street 2012)

FULLER, LON, *THE MORALITY OF LAW* (Yale 1969)

Galliher, Keys & Elsner, *Lindesmith v. Anslinger: An Early Government Victory in the Failed War on Drugs*, JOURNAL OF CRIMINAL LAW AND CRIMINOLOGY Vol. 88:681 (1998)

Gerber, Scott D., *Liberal Originalism: The Declaration of Independence and Constitutional Interpretation*, CLEVELAND STATE LAW REVIEW Vol. 63:1 (2014)

GERBER, SCOTT D., *TO SECURE THESE RIGHTS* (New York 1995)

Gershowitz, Adam M., *An Informational Approach to the Mass Imprisonment Problem*, FACULTY PUBLICATIONS, Paper 1264 (2008)

GEWIRTH, ALAN, *THE COMMUNITY OF RIGHTS* (Chicago 1996)

GEWIRTH, ALAN, *REASON AND MORALITY* (Chicago 1981)

Goldberg, Suzanne B., *Equality Without Tiers*, SOUTHERN CALIFORNIA LAW REVIEW Vol. 77:481 (2004)

Gowder, Paul, *Equal Law in an Unequal World*, IOWA LAW REVIEW Vol. 99:1021 (2014)

GRAY, CHRISTOPHER, *THE ACID DIARIES: A PSYCHONAUT'S GUIDE TO THE HISTORY AND USE OF LSD* (Park Street 2010)

GRAY, JAMES P., *WHY OUR DRUG LAWS HAVE FAILED AND WHAT WE CAN DO ABOUT IT: A JUDICIAL INDICTMENT OF THE WAR ON DRUGS* (Temple 2001)

Grey, Thomas C., *The Uses of an Unwritten Constitution*, CHICAGO-KENT LAW REVIEW Vol. 64:211 (1988)

GRINSPOON, LESTER, *MARIJUANA RECONSIDERED* (Harvard 1977)

GRITZ, JAMES BO, *A NATION BETRAYED* (Lazarus 1989)

Grob, Charles et al., *Pilot Study of Psilocybin Treatment for Anxiety in Patients with Advanced-stage Cancer*, ARCHIVES OF GENERAL PSYCHIATRY Vol. 68, no. 1 (2011)

GROF, STANISLAV, *THE COSMIC GAME: EXPLORATIONS OF THE FRONTIERS OF HUMAN CONSCIOUSNESS* (Suny 1998)

GROF, STANISLAV, *LSD: DOORWAY TO THE NUMINOUS* (Park Street 2009)

GROF, STANISLAV, *REALMS OF THE HUMAN UNCONSCIOUS: OBSERVATIONS FROM LSD RESEARCH* (Souvenir 1979)

GROF, STANISLAV & HALIFAX, JOAN, *THE HUMAN ENCOUNTER WITH DEATH* (Dutton 1977)

Grosman, Lucas S., *Drugs under the Constitution*, SELA PAPERS, Paper 108 (2012)

Grund, Jean-Paul & Breeksema, Joost, *Coffee Shops and Compromise: Separated Illicit Drug Markets in the Netherlands*, OPEN SOCIETY FOUNDATIONS (2013)

Gunther, Gerald, Foreword: *In Search of Evolving Doctrine on a Changing Court: A Model for a Newer Equal Protection*, HARVARD LAW REVIEW Vol. 86:1 (1972)

Gur-Arye, Miriam & Weigend, Thomas, *Constitutional Review of Criminal Prohibitions Affecting Human Dignity and Liberty: German and Israeli Perspectives*, ISRAELI LAW REVIEW Vol. 44:63 (2011)

Hallam, Bewley-Taylor, & Jelsma, *Scheduling in the International Drug Control System*, SERIES ON LEGISLATIVE REFORM OF DRUG POLICIES No. 25 (2014)

Hamburger, Philip A., *Natural Rights, Natural Law & American Constitutions*, YALE LAW JOURNAL Vol. 102: 907 (1993)

HANCOCK, GRAHAM (ED.), *THE DIVINE SPARK: PSYCHEDELICS, CONSCIOUSNESS AND THE BIRTH OF CIVILIZATION* (HayHouse 2015)

HART, CARL, *HIGH PRICE* (Harper 2014)

Hart, Henry M., *The Aims of the Criminal Law*, LAW AND CONTEMPORARY PROBLEMS Vol. 23:401 (1958)

HARTSTEIN, MAX, *THE WAR ON DRUGS: THE WORST ADDICTION OF ALL* (2003)

Hessick, Andrew, *Rethinking the Presumption of Constitutionality*, NOTRE DAME LAW REVIEW Vol. 85:1447 (2010)

Heyman, Steven J., *The First Duty of Government: Protection, Liberty, and the Fourteenth Amendment*, DUKE LAW JOURNAL 41:507 (1991)

Hindes, Thomas L., *Morality Enforcement Through the Criminal Law and the Modern Doctrine of Substantive Due Process*, UNIVERSITY OF PENNSYLVANIA LAW REVIEW Vol. 126:344 (1977)

Hirschl, Ran, *The Rise of Comparative Constitutional Law: Thoughts on substance and Method*, INDIAN JOURNAL OF CONSTITUTIONAL LAW (2008)

HOBBES, THOMAS, *LEVIATHAN* (Penguin 1982)

Holmes, Justice, *Common Carriers and the Common Law*, THE ANGLO-AMERICAN LAW REVIEW Vol. 13:609 (1879)

Hughes, Jula, *Restraint and Proliferation in criminal Law*, REVIEW OF CONSTITUTIONAL STUDIES Vol. 15, Issue 1 (2010)

Huhn, Wilson, *The Jurisprudential Revolution: Unlocking Human Potential in Grutter and Lawrence*, WILLIAM & MARY BILL OF RIGHTS JOURNAL Vol. 12:65 (2004)

Husak, Douglas, *Applying Ultima Ratio: A Skeptical Assessment*, OHIO STATE JOURNAL OF CRIMINAL LAW Vol. 2:535 (2005)

HUSAK, DOUGLAS, *DRUGS AND RIGHTS* (Cambridge 1996)

Husak, Douglas, *Four Points about Drug Decriminalization*, CRIMINAL JUSTICE ETHICS Vol. 22, Issue 1 (2003)

HUSAK, DOUGLAS, *LEGALIZE THIS! THE CASE FOR DECRIMINALIZING DRUGS* (Verso 2002)

Husak, Douglas, *Liberal Neutrality, Autonomy, and Drug Prohibitions*, PHILOSOPHY AND PUBLIC AFFAIRS Vol. 29, No. 1 (2000)

HUSAK, DOUGLAS, *OVERCRIMINALIZATION: THE LIMITS OF THE CRIMINAL LAW* (Oxford 2008)

HUSAK, DOUGLAS & DE MARNEFFE, PETER, *THE LEGALIZATION OF DRUGS: FOR AND AGAINST* (Cambridge 2005)

Jackson, Jeffrey D., *Putting Rationality Back Into the Rational Basis Test: Saving Substantive Due Process and Redeeming the Promise of the Ninth Amendment*, UNIVERSITY OF RICHMOND LAW REVIEW Vol. 45:491 (2011)

Jackson, Vicki C., *Constitutional Law in an Age of Proportionality*, YALE LAW REVIEW Vol. 124:3094 (2015)

JEFFERSON, THOMAS, *THE ANAS* (Online book)

Jelsma, Martin, *Drugs in the UN system: The Unwritten History of the 1998 United Nations General Assembly Special Session on Drugs*, INTERNATIONAL JOURNAL OF DRUG POLICY Vol. 14 (2003)

Kadish, Sanford H., *The Crisis of Overcriminalization*, AMERICAN CRIMINAL LAW QUARTERLY Vol.7:17 (1968)

Kadish, Sanford H., *Fifty Years of Criminal Law: An Opinionated Review*, CALIFORNIA LAW REVIEW Vol. 87: 943 (1999)

KAPLAN, JOHN, *MARIJUANA: THE NEW PROHIBITION* (Pocket Books 1971)

Kaplan, John, *The Role of Law in Drug Control: Self-Harming Conduct and Society*, DUKE LAW JOURNAL Vol. 1971:1065 (1971)

Karlan, Pamela S., *Equal Protection, Due Process and the Stereoscopic Fourteenth Amendment*, MCGEORGE LAW REVIEW Vol. 33:473 (2002)

Karst, Kenneth L., *The Liberties of Equal Citizens: Groups and the Due Process Clause*, UCLA LAW REVIEW Vol. 55:99 (2007)

Kesavan & Stokes, *The Interpretive Force of the Constitution's Secret Drafting History*, GEORGIA LAW JOURNAL Vol. 91:1112 (2003)

KING, RUFUS, *THE DRUG HANG UP: AMERICA'S FIFTY-YEAR FOLLY* (Norton 1972)

King, Rufus, *Wild Shots in the War on Crime*, JOURNAL OF PUBLIC LAW Vol. 20:85 (1971)

Kumm, Mattias, *Democracy is not enough: Rights, proportionality and the point of judicial review*, NEW YORK UNIVERSITY PUBLIC LAW AND LEGAL THEORY WORKING PAPERS, Paper 118 (2009)

Kumm, Mattias, *The Idea of Socratic Contestation and the Right to Justification: The Point of Rights-Based Proportionality Review*, LAW & ETHICS OF HUMAN RIGHTS Vol. 4:141 (2010)

KURLAND, PHILIP & LERNER, RALPH, *THE FOUNDERS' CONSTITUTION* (Online book)

KWITNY, JONATHAN, *THE CRIMES OF PATRIOTS: A TRUE TALE OF DOPE, DIRTY MONEY, AND THE CIA* (Norton 1987)

LANGER, ELLEN & ALEXANDER, CHARLES, *HIGHER STAGES OF HUMAN DEVELOPMENT: PERSPECTIVES ON ADULT GROWTH* (Oxford 1990)

Laniel, Laurent, *The Relationship between Research and Drug Policy in the United States*, MANAGEMENT OF SOCIAL TRANSFORMATIONS, Discussion Paper No. 44 (1999)

Lash, Kurt, *The Lost History of the Ninth Amendment: The Lost Original Meaning*, LOYOLA LAW SCHOOL, Research Paper No. 2004-5 (2004)

Lee, Donna, *Resuscitating Proportionality in Noncapital Criminal Sentencing*, ARIZONA STATE LAW JOURNAL Vol. 40:527 (2008)

Lee, Youngjae, *The Constitutional Right Against Excessive Punishment*, NEW YORK UNIVERSITY PUBLIC LAW AND LEGAL THEORY Working Papers, Paper 3 (2005)

Levinson, Daryl J., *Empire-Building Government in Constitutional Law*, NYU LAW SCHOOL PUBLIC LAW AND LEGAL THEORY Working Paper Series, Working Paper No. 84 (2004)

Levinson, Rosalie Berger, *Reining in Abuses of Executive Power through Substantive Due Process*, FLORIDA LAW REVIEW Vol. 60:519 (2008)

LOCKE, JOHN, *TWO TREATIES OF GOVERNMENT AND A LETTER CONCERNING TOLERATION* (Yale 2003)

Luna, Erik, *The Overcriminalization Phenomenon*, AMERICAN UNIVERSITY LAW REVIEW Vol. 54:703 (2005)

MAAS, PETER, *MANHUNT* (Randomhouse1986)

MACCOUN, ROBERT & REUTER, PETER, *DRUG WAR HERESIES* (Cambridge 2001)

MADISON, HAMILTON & JAY, *THE FEDERALIST PAPERS* (Timeless Classics 2010)

Maguire, Sarah A. & Nourse, V.F, *The Lost History of Governance and Equal Protection*, DUKE LAW JOURNAL Vol. 58:955 (2009)

MARTIN, AL, *THE CONSPIRATORS: SECRETS OF AN IRAN-CONTRA INSIDER* (National Liberty 2002)

MASLOW, ABRAHAM, *RELIGIONS, VALUES, AND PEAK-EXPERIENCES* (Penguin 1994)

MASLOW, ABRAHAM, *TOWARD A PSYCHOLOGY OF BEING* (Van Nostrand 1982)

Massey, Calvin, *The New Formalism: Requiem for Tiered Scrutiny?* UNIVERSITY OF PENNSYLVANIA JOURNAL OF CONSTITUTIONAL LAW Vol. 6:945 (2004)

MASTERS, BILL, *DRUG WAR ADDICTION: NOTES FROM THE FRONTLINES OF AMERICA'S NO. 1 POLICY DISASTER* (Accurate 2001)

Materni, Mike C., *The 100-plus Year Old Case for a Minimalist Criminal Law*, NEW CRIMINAL LAW REVIEW Vol. 18 issue 3 (2015)

MATHRE, M.L., *CANNABIS IN MEDICAL PRACTICE: A LEGAL, HISTORICAL, AND PHARMACOLOGICAL OVERVIEW OF THE THERAPEUTIC USE OF MARIJUANA* (McFarland 1997)

Mazur, Cynthia S., *Marijuana as a Holy Sacrament: Is the Issue of Peyote Constitutionally Distinguishable from That of Marijuana in Bona Fide Religious Ceremonies?* NOTRE DAME LAW REVIEW Vol. 5:693 (1991)

MAZUR, ROBERT, *THE INFILTRATOR* (Little Brown 2009)

McAffee, Thomas B., *The Original Meaning of the Ninth Amendment*, COLOMBIA LAW REVIEW Vol. 90:1215 (1990)

McConnell, Michael W., *Natural Rights and the Ninth Amendment: How Does Lockean Legal Theory Assist in Interpretation?* NYU JOURNAL OF LAW AND LIBERTY Vol. 5:1 (2010)

MCDONALD, FORREST, *NOVUS ORDO SECLORUM: THE INTELLECTUAL ORIGINS OF THE CONSTITUTION* (Kansas 1985)

McGinnis, John & Mulaney, Charles, *Judging Facts Like Law: The Courts Versus Congress in Social Fact-Finding*, CONSTITUTIONAL COMMENTARY Vol. 25, Issue 1 (2008)

MCWHIRTER, DARIEN & BIBLE, JON, *PRIVACY AS A CONSTITUTIONAL RIGHT: SEX, DRUGS, AND THE RIGHT TO LIFE* (Quorum 1992)

MENASHE, ARI BEN, *PROFITS OF WAR: INSIDE THE SECRET US ISRAELI ARMS NETWORK* (Sheridan 1998)

MIKALSEN, ROAR, *REASON IS: ON THE NATURE OF CONSCIOUSNESS AND HOW EVERYTHING IS CONNECTED TO EVERYTHING* (Createspace 2014)

MIKALSEN, ROAR, *TO END A WAR: A SHORT HISTORY OF HUMAN RIGHTS, THE RULE OF LAW, AND HOW DRUG PROHIBITION VIOLATES THE BILL OF RIGHTS* (Createspace 2015)

MIKALSEN, ROAR, *TO RIGHT A WRONG: A TRANSPERSONAL FRAMEWORK FOR CONSTITUTIONAL INTERPRETATION* (Createspace 2016)

MILL, JOHN STUART, *ON LIBERTY* (Hackett 1978)

MILLER, RICHARD LAWRENCE, *THE CASE FOR LEGALIZING DRUGS* (Praeger 1991)

MILLER, RICHARD LAWRENCE, *DRUG WARRIORS AND THEIR PREY: FROM POLICE POWER TO POLICE STATE* (Praeger 1996)

MILLS, JAMES, *THE UNDERGROUND EMPIRE: WHERE CRIME AND GOVERNMENTS EMBRACE* (Doubleday 1986)

MÖLLER, KAI, *THE GLOBAL MODEL OF CONSTITUTIONAL RIGHTS* (Oxford 2012)

Möller, Kai, *Proportionality: Challenging the critics*, I.CON Vol. 10: 709 (2012)

MUSTO, DAVID, *THE AMERICAN DISEASE: ORIGINS OF NARCOTIC CONTROL* (Yale 1973)

Nelson, Caleb, *Judicial Review and Legislative Purpose*, NEW YORK UNIVERSITY LAW REVIEW Vol. 83:1784 (2008)

Nelson, William E., *Changing Conceptions of Judicial Review: The Evolution of Constitutional Theory in the United States 1790-1860*, UNIVERSITY OF PENNSYLVANIA LAW REVIEW Vol. 120:1166 (1972)

Niles, Mark C., *Ninth Amendment Adjudication: An Alternative to Substantive Due Process Analysis of Personal Autonomy Rights*, UCLA LAW REVIEW Vol. 48:85 (2000)

Nilsen, Eva & Blumenson, Eric, *Liberty Lost: The Moral Case for Marijuana Law Reform*, SUFFOLK UNIVERSITY LAW SCHOOL, Research Paper No. 09-20 (2009)

Nilsen, Eva & Blumenson, Eric, *Policing for Profit: The Drug War's Hidden Economic Agenda*, UNIVERSITY OF CHICAGO LAW REVIEW Vol. 65:35 (1998)

NORMAND, ROGER & ZAIDI, SARAH, *HUMAN RIGHTS AT THE UN: THE POLITICAL HISTORY OF UNIVERSAL JUSTICE* (Indiana 2008)

NUTT, DAVID, *DRUGS—WITHOUT THE HOT AIR: MINIMISING THE HARMS OF LEGAL AND ILLEGAL DRUGS* (Cambridge 2012)

O'BRIEN, KATHY, *TRANCE-FORMATION OF AMERICA* (Reality 1995)

O'Scannlain, Diarmuid F., *The Natural Law in the American Tradition*, FORDHAM LAW REVIEW Vol. 79:1513 (2011)

Ostrowski, James, *Answering the Critics of Drug Legalization*, NOTRE DAME JOURNAL OF LAW, ETHICS & PUBLIC POLICY Vol. 5:823 (1991)

Ostrowski, James, *The Moral and Practical Case for Drug Legalization,* HOFSTRA LAW REVIEW Vol. 18: Issue 3, Article 5 (1990)

Oteri & Silvergate, *The Pursuit of Pleasure: Constitutional Dimensions of the Marihuana Problem*, SUFFOLK LAW REVIEW Vol. 3:55 (1968)

PACKER, HERBERT L., *THE LIMITS OF THE CRIMINAL SANCTION* (Stanford 1968)

PEIKOFF, LEONARD, *THE OMINOUS PARALLELS* (New American Library 1982)

PAINE, THOMAS, *RIGHTS OF MAN* (WordsWorth 1996)

Preiser, Peter, *Rediscovering a Coherent Rationale for Substantive Due Process*, MARQUETTE LAW REVIEW Vol. 87:1 (2003)

PROVINE, DORIS MARIE, *UNEQUAL UNDER LAW: RACE IN THE WAR ON DRUGS* (Chicago 2007)

RAWLS, JOHN, *A THEORY OF JUSTICE* (Harvard 2003)

RAWLS, JOHN, *JUSTICE AS FAIRNESS: A RESTATEMENT* (Harvard 2003)

REED, TERRY & CUMMINGS, JOHN, *COMPROMISED: CLINTON, BUSH AND THE CIA* (SPI 1994)

Reinarman, Craig, Cohen Peter D. A., & Kaal, Hendrien L., *The Limited Relevance of Drug Policy: Cannabis in Amsterdam and in San Francisco*, AMERICAN JOURNAL OF PUBLIC HEALTH Vol. 94:836 (2004)

Reynolds, Glenn &. Kopel, David, *The Evolving Police Power: Some Observations for a New Century*, HASTINGS CONSTITUTIONAL LAW QUARTERLY Vol. 27:511 (2000)

Richards, David A. J., *Human Rights and the Moral Foundations of the Substantive Criminal Law*, GEORGIA LAW REVIEW 13:1395 (1978)

Richards, David A.J., *Liberalism, Public Morality, and Constitutional Law: Prolegomenon to a Theory of the Constitutional Right to Privacy*, LAW AND CONTEMPORARY PROBLEMS Vol. 51:123 (1988)

RICHARDS, DAVID A.J., *SEX, DRUGS, DEATH, AND THE LAW: AN ESSAY ON HUMAN RIGHTS AND OVERCRIMINALIZATION* (Rowman 1982)

RICHARDS, DAVID A. J., *TOLERATION AND THE CONSTITUTION* (Oxford 1989)

Richards, David A.J., *Unnatural Acts and the Constitutional Right to Privacy: A Moral Theory*, FORDHAM LAW REVIEW Vol. 45:1281 (1977)

Roach, Kent, *The Primacy of Liberty and Proportionality, Not Human Dignity, When Subjecting Criminal Law to Constitutional Control*, ISRAELI LAW REVIEW Vol. 44:91 (2011)

Robinson, Paul H. & Darley, John M., *The Utility of Desert*, NORTHWESTERN UNIVERSITY LAW REVIEW Vol. 91:453 (1997)

ROBINSON, MATTHEW & SCHERLEN, RENEE, *LIES, DAMN LIES, AND DRUG WAR STATISTICS* (SUNY 2007)

ROOM, ROBIN, ET AL., *CANNABIS POLICY: MOVING BEYOND STALEMATE* (Oxford 2010)

Rosenfeld, Michel, *The Rule of Law and the Legitimacy of Constitutional Democracy*, SOUTHERN CALIFORNIA LAW REVIEW Vol. 74:1307 (2001)

ROUSSEAU, JEAN-JACQUES, *THE SOCIAL CONTRACT* (Digireads 2005)

Rubin, Edward L., *Bureaucratic Oppression: It's Causes and Cures*, VANDERBILT UNIVERSITY LAW SCHOOL, Working Paper no. 14-15 (2012)

Rubin, Edward, *Judicial Review and the Right to Resist*, VANDERBILT UNIVERSITY LAW SCHOOL, Working Paper Number 08-11 (2008)

RUPPERT, MIKE, *CROSSING THE RUBICON: THE DECLINE OF THE AMERICAN EMPIRE AT THE END OF THE AGE OF OIL* (NEW SOCIETY 2004)

RUSSELL, DAN, *DRUG WAR: COVERT MONEY, POWER AND POLICY* (Kalyx 2000)

Sabo, Michael, *The Higher Law Background of the Constitution: Justice Clarence Thomas and Constitutional Interpretation,* ASHBROOK STATESMANSHIP THESIS (2009)

Sanders, Chase J., *Ninth Life: An Interpretive Theory of the Ninth Amendment*, INDIANA LAW JOURNAL Vol. 69:759 (1994)

Santiago, Miriam Defensor, *The New Equal Protection*, PHILIPPINE LAW JOURNAL Vol. 58:1 (1983)

SCHALER, JEFFREY (ED.), *DRUGS: SHOULD WE LEGALIZE, DECRIMINALIZE OR DEREGULATE?* (Prometheus 1998)

SCOTT, PETER DALE, *AMERICAN WAR MACHINE: DEEP POLITICS, THE CIA GLOBAL DRUG CONNECTION, AND THE ROAD TO AFGHANISTAN* (Rowman 2014)

SEN, AMARTYA, *THE IDEA OF JUSTICE* (Harvard 2011)

Shedler, Jonathan & Block, Jack, *Adolescent Drug Use and Psychological Health: A Longitudinal Inquiry*, AMERICAN PSYCHOLOGIST Vol. 45 (1990)

Sherry, Suzana, *The Founders' Unwritten Constitution*, UNIVERSITY OF CHICAGO LAW REVIEW Vol. 54:1127 (1987)

Sherry, Suzanna, *The Ninth Amendment: Righting an Unwritten Constitution*, CHICAGO-KENT LAW REVIEW Vol. 64:1001 (1988)

SHULGIN, ALEXANDER, *PIKHAL: A CHEMICAL LOVE STORY* (Transform 1992)

Siegel, Stephen A., *The Origin of the Compelling State Interest Test and Strict Scrutiny*, AMERICAN JOURNAL OF LEGAL HISTORY Vol. 48:355 (2006)

SIMON, STEPHEN A., *HUMAN RIGHTS OR AMERICAN PRIVILEGES? THE SUPREME COURT'S EVOLVING USE OF UNIVERSAL REASONING* (Doctoral dissertation 2007)

Smith, Annaliese, Comment, *Marijuana as a Schedule I Substance: Political Ploy or Accepted Science?* SANTA CLARA LAW REVIEW Vol. 40:1137 (2000)

SMITH, HUSTON, *CLEANSING THE DOORS OF PERCEPTION: THE RELIGIOUS SIGNIFICANCE OF ENTHEOGENIC PLANTS AND CHEMICALS* (Tarcher/Putnam 2000)

Snure, Brian, *A Frequent Recurrence to Fundamental Principles: Individual Rights, Free Government, and the Washington State Constitution*, WASHINGTON LAW REVIEW Vol. 67:669 (1992)

Solum, Lawrence B., *Originalism and the Unwritten Constitution*, UNIVERSITY OF ILLINOIS LAW REVIEW Vol. 2013:1935 (2013)

Spooner, Lysander, *Vices are Not Crimes: a Vindication of Moral Liberty* (1875) (Online book)

Stevens, Alex, *Drug Policy, Harm and Human Rights: A Rationalist Approach*, INTERNATIONAL JOURNAL OF DRUG POLICY 22 (2011)

STICH, RODNEY, *DEFRAUDING AMERICA* (Diablo 1988)

STOLAROFF, M.J., *THANATOS TO EROS: THIRTY-FIVE YEARS OF PSYCHEDELIC EXPLORATION* (VWB 1994)

STRASSMAN, RICK, *DMT AND THE SOUL OF PROPHECY: A NEW SCIENCE OF SPIRITUAL REVELATION IN THE HEBREW BIBLE* (Park Street 2014)

Stuart, Susan, *War as Metaphor and the Rule of Law in Crisis: The Lessons We Should Have Learned from the War on Drugs*, VALPARASIO UNIVERSITY SCHOOL OF LAW, Legal Studies Research Paper (2011)

STUNTZ, WILLIAM J., *THE COLLAPSE OF AMERICAN CRIMINAL JUSTICE* (Harvard 2013)

Stuntz, William J., *The Pathological Politics of Criminal Law*, HARVARD LAW SCHOOL Public Law Working Paper No. 22 (2001)

Sun, Tammy W., *Equality by Other Means: The Substantive Foundations of the Vagueness Doctrine*, HARVARD CIVIL RIGHTS-CIVIL LIBERTIES LAW REVIEW Vol. 46:150 (2011)

Sunstein, Cass R., *Homosexuality and the Constitution*, INDIANA LAW JOURNAL Vol. 70:1 (1994)

Sweet, Alec S., *All Things in Proportion? American Rights Doctrine and the Problem of Balancing*, Faculty Scholarship Series Paper 30 (2010)

SZASZ, THOMAS, *CEREMONIAL CHEMISTRY: THE RITUAL PERSECUTION OF DRUGS, ADDICTS, AND PUSHERS* (Syracuse University 2003)

SZASZ, THOMAS, *OUR RIGHT TO DRUGS: THE CASE FOR A FREE MARKET* (Praeger 1992)

TAILOR, JOHN, *CONSTRUCTION CONSTRUED AND CONSTITUTIONS VINDICATED* (1820) (Online book)

TART, CHARLES L., *TRANSPERSONAL PSYCHOLOGIES: PERSPECTIVES ON THE MIND FROM SEVEN GREAT SPIRITUAL TRADITIONS* (Harper 1992)

Tennen, Eric, *Is the Constitution in Harm's Way? Substantive Due Process and Criminal Law*, BOALT JOURNAL OF CRIMINAL LAW Vol. 8: 3 (2004)

Thomas, Clarence, *Judging*, UNIVERSITY OF KANSAS LAW REVIEW Vol. 45:1 (1996)

Thomas, Clarence, Toward a Plain Reading of the Constitution: The Declaration of Independence in Constitutional Interpretation, HOWARD LAW JOURNAL Vol. 30:691 (1987)

Torke, James W., *the Judicial Process in Equal Protection Cases*, HASTINGS CONSTITUTIONAL LAW QUARTERLY Vol. 9:279 (1982)

Treiman, David M., *Equal Protection and Fundamental Rights—A Judicial Shell Game*, TULSA LAW REVIEW Vol. 15:183 (1979)

Tribe, Laurence H., *Lawrence v. Texas: The Fundamental Right that Dare Not Speak its Name*, HARVARD LAW REVIEW Vol. 117:1893 (2004)

Tribe, Laurence H., *On Reading the Constitution*, The Tanner Lectures on Human Values, Delivered at The University of Utah (November 17 and 18, 1986)

Tribe, Laurence H., *Reflections on Unenumerated Rights*, JOURNAL OF CONSTITUTIONAL LAW Vol. 9:483 (2007)

Tribe, Laurence & Dorf, Michael, *Levels of Generality in the Definition of Rights*, UNIVERSITY OF CHICAGO LAW REVIEW Vol. 57:1057 (1990)

Tupper, Kenneth & Labate, Beatriz, *Plants, Psychoactive Substances and the International Narcotics Control Board: The Control of Nature and the Nature of Control*, HUMAN RIGHTS AND DRUGS Vol. 2 No 1 (2012)

Tussman, Jospeh & tenBroek, Jacobus, *The Equal Protection of the Laws*, CALIFORNIA LAW REVIEW Vol. 37:341 (1949)

UNDP, *Perspectives on the Development Dimensions of Drug Control Policy* (March 2015)

VALENTINE, DOUGLAS, *THE STRENGTH OF THE WOLF* (Verso 2004)

Vollenweider, Franz X. & Kometer, Michael, *The Neurobiology of Psychedelic Drugs: Implications for the Treatment of Mood Disorders*, NATURE REVIEWS NEUROSCIENCE Vol. 11 (2010)

WADE, JENNY, *CHANGES OF MIND: A HOLONOMIC THEORY OF THE EVOLUTION OF CONSCIOUSNESS* (State university of New York Press 1996)

WALSH, ROGER N., & VAUGHAN, FRANCES, *BEYOND EGO: TRANSPERSONAL DIMENSIONS IN PSYCHOLOGY* (Tarcher 1980)

Ward, Andrew, *The Rational Basis Test Violates Due Process*, NYU JOURNAL OF LAW & LIBERTY Vol. 8:713 (2014)

Werb et al., *Effect of Drug Law Enforcement on Drug-Related Violence: Evidence from a Scientific Review*, INTERNATIONAL CENTRE FOR SCIENCE IN DRUG POLICY (2010)

West, Robin, *The Authoritarian Impulse in Constitutional Law*, UNIVERSITY OF MIAMI LAW REVIEW Vol. 42: 531 (1988)

WILBER, KEN, *THE EYE OF SPIRIT: AN INTEGRAL VISION FOR A WORLD GONE SLIGHTLY MAD* (Shambala 1998).

WILBER, KEN, *EYE TO EYE: THE QUEST FOR THE NEW PARADIGM* (Shambala 1996).

WILBER, KEN, *INTEGRAL SPIRITUALITY: A STARTLING NEW ROLE FOR RELIGION IN THE MODERN AND POSTMODERN WORLD* (Integral Books 2006).

WILBER, KEN, *UP FROM EDEN: A TRANSPERSONAL VIEW OF HUMAN EVOLUTION* (New Science Library 1986).

WILBER, KEN, *QUANTUM QUESTIONS: MYSTICAL WRITINGS OF THE WORLD'S GREATEST PHYSICISTS* (Shambala 2001).

WILLIAMS, PAUL, *OPERATION GLADIO: THE UNTOLD STORY OF THE UNHOLY ALLIANCE BETWEEN THE VATICAN, THE CIA, AND THE MAFIA* (Prometheus 2015)

WILKINSON, RICHARD & PICKETT, KATE, *THE SPIRIT LEVEL: WHY EQUALITY IS BETTER FOR EVERYONE* (Penguin 2010).

Williams, Ryan C., *The One and Only Substantive Due Process Clause*, THE YALE LAW JOURNAL Vol. 120:408 (2010)

WINKELMAN, MICHAEL & ROBERTS, THOMAS (EDS.), *PSYCHEDELIC MEDICINE: NEW EVIDENCE FOR HALLUCINOGENIC SUBSTANCES AS TREATMENTS* (Praeger 2007)

Winterbourne, Matt, *United States drug policy: The Scientific, Economic, and Social Issues Surrounding Marijuana* (2012)

Wisotsky, Steven, *A Society of Suspects: The War on Drugs and Civil Liberties*, CATO POLICY ANALYSIS No. 180 (1992)

WISOTSKY, STEVEN, *BEYOND THE WAR ON DRUGS: OVERCOMING A FAILED PUBLIC POLICY* (Prometheus 1990)

Wisotsky, Steven, *Not thinking Like a Lawyer: The Case of Drugs in the Courts*, NOTRE DAME JOURNAL OF LAW, ETHICS AND PUBLIC POLICY, Volume 5, Issue No. 3 (1991)

WOLLSTONECRAFT, MARY, *A VINDICATION OF THE RIGHTS OF MAN* (1792) (Online book)

WOLLSTONECRAFT, MARY, *A VINDICATION OF THE RIGHTS OF WOMAN* (Online Library of Liberty 1790)

Yankah, Ekow N., *A Paradox in Overcriminalization*, NEW CRIMINAL LAW REVIEW Vol. 14:1 (2011)

Yoshino, Kenji, *The New Equal Protection*, HARVARD LAW REVIEW Vol. 124:747 (2011)

ZIMBARDO, PHILIP, *THE LUCIFER EFFECT: HOW GOOD PEOPLE TURN EVIL* (Rider 2009)

About the author

Roar Mikalsen is the author of six books which are changing the world one at a time. His authorship covers a large area ranging from cosmology, mysticism, self-help, and consciousness research to power politics, human rights law, drug policy, constitutional interpretation, and social engineering. He is the founder of the Alliance for Rights-Oriented Drug Policies (AROD), an organization which addresses drug policy reform from a perspective of human rights and a nominee of two prestigious human rights awards (Vaclav Havel and Martin Ennals).

A platform for his work is Life Liberty Productions, a publishing house and consulting agency dedicated to the Spirit of Freedom. You will find books that are embraced by professionals and have the potential to bring humanity one step further on the online store lifelibertybooks.com